Winnie-the-Pooh
on Management
& Problem Solving

Winnie-the-Pooh on Management & Problem Solving

ROGER E. ALLEN & STEPHEN D. ALLEN

METHUEN

First published in Great Britain 1998
Printed under the Methuen imprint
by Egmont Children's Books Limited
239 Kensington High Street, London W8 6SL
Copyright © 1998 Roger E. Allen and Stephen E. Allen
The authors have asserted their moral rights

Winnie-the-Pooh on Management by Roger E. Allen
first published in Great Britain in 1995
Copyright © 1994 Roger E. Allen
Published in arrangement with Dutton Signet, a division of Penguin Books USA, Inc

Winnie-the-Pooh on Problem Solving by Roger E. Allen and Stephen D. Allen
first published in Great Britain in 1997
Copyright © 1995 Roger E. Allen and Stephen D. Allen
Published in arrangement with Dutton Signet, a division of Penguine Books USA, Inc

Text by A.A. Milne and illustrations by E.H. Shepard
from *Winnie-the-Pooh* and *The House at Pooh Corner*
copyright under the Berne Convention
Grateful acknowledgement is made to the Trustees of the Pooh Properties
for the use of quoted material by A.A. Milne and illustrations by E.H. Shepard

The SOLVE problem-solving method
copyright © Allen Associates 1991
Allen Associates Productivity Workshop

A CIP catalogue record for this book is available from the British Library

ISBN 0 416 19513 X

3 5 7 9 10 8 6 4 2

Printed and bound in Great Britain

Winnie-the-Pooh
on Management

This book is dedicated to:

Marilyn: my friend, my wife, my love, my life.

Our three sons and their families:
Mark, his wife, Jody, Matt and Scottie
Stephen, his wife, Stasia, Christopher and Thomas
Jeffrey, his wife, Shirley, and Bryce.

ACKNOWLEDGMENTS

A book is a collaborative effort, even if the author's name stands alone on the title page. I want to express my appreciation and thanks to those who helped make this book possible.

Winnie-the-Pooh, a Very Important Bear

Steve Allen

Stasia Allen

Marilyn G. Allen

Mark E. Allen

Jeff Allen

Esther J. Allen: my mother, who told me stories and introduced me to Edward Bear

The staff of Dutton, including:

Rachel Klayman and Matthew Carnicelli, my editors; Julie Park, Joan Powers, Lisa Johnson, and others.

And, of course, A. A. Milne, creator of children's classics.

And all the managers, good and bad, with whom I have worked. I learned from every one of you.

CONTENTS

INTRODUCTION

. . . Christopher Robin said:
"What do you like doing best in the world, Pooh?"
"Well," said Pooh, "what I like best—" and then he
had to stop and think. Because although Eating Honey was
a very good thing to do, there was a moment just before you
began to eat it which was better than when you were, but he
didn't know what it was called.

If you were reading a good book, that moment might be called an "Introduction." Ideally, it should raise your anticipation, tell you what the book is about, how it came to be written, and why you should read it.

All about us we can see failures of management: unrepaired potholes, high school graduates who can't read or write, cars that need to be recalled, wasted tax dollars, unsafe streets and neighborhoods. The list is long and increases daily. Why is this?

My management experience in both the private and public sector has convinced me that managers need to spend less time and attention on sophisticated approaches to management and devote more time to improving and practicing the six functions of a manager's job. They need to get back to basics.

That is what this book is about—the six functions that a manager should master, and how every manager can do so.

The book is also about A. A. Milne's world of Winnie-the-Pooh. At first it might seem odd to combine a children's classic with management. The purpose of doing so is to explore the six functions in an unfamiliar context, which will allow us to think about them in a new way and make the basics of a manager's job clear and understandable.

If this is to be done, one or more visits to that world would be "REQIRD" (as Owl's door knocker's notice read) to refresh memories of Pooh's adventures and to see what we can learn from them.

It has been a long time since I visited the Forest where Pooh and his friends live. I would be a stranger there to be sure, but I am certain that Pooh will help, being That Kind of Bear.

If you are a manager, there may be some reminders in this book about things you know but haven't thought about recently and some skills that could stand a little honing and polishing.

If you'd like to be a manager but aren't, this is a good place to start.

If you aren't a manager, the skills of a manager can help you manage your own day-to-day activities better.

If you're a significant other, child, spouse, or friend

of a manager, this book can help you to understand the Very Important Job a manager does.

So, follow along on tiptoe to the Forest and see what adventures await. Don't worry about finding it. After all, A. A. Milne said in his introduction to *The House At Pooh Corner* ". . . the Forest will always be there . . . and anybody who is Friendly with Bears can find it."

Come. . . .

I

In which Winnie-the-Pooh Learns About Management and What Makes Someone a Manager

That morning Pooh had been looking in the Forest for a bee-tree that might possibly contain honey, when he came up behind a stranger standing still and looking as if he might be lost.

Pooh had had some experience in being lost the time they had tried to unBounce Tigger. He knew how offputting it could be when you've missed your way somehow, so he spoke up nicely.

"Hallo," he said in his best I-know-where-I-am voice, just to be reassuring. "I'm Edward Bear. Can I help you?"

The Stranger turned around, stopped looking lost, and looked pleased. "Good morning, Pooh. I was hoping to find you so that you could. Help me, that is."

"How could I help you?" asked Pooh.

"Well." The Stranger put down the picnic basket he

had been holding. "I'm writing a book, and it seemed to me that if you let me write about some of the adventures you and your friends have had, it would be a better book. It's a book about management."

"Man-age-ment," said Edward Bear in the somewhat puzzled tone he used when he was thinking, or, as Eeyore might say, "Trying to think."

"Yes. Management."

"That is a very long word." Pooh reflected. "It is the kind of long word that Owl uses. Does it stand for something good, like ah ummm honey?"

"Well, not exactly. It stands for something that some people called managers do. Management is neither good nor bad. It just is. You can have either good or bad management, depending on how managers do their job."

"That seems very confusing. Almost everyone I know thinks that honey is good always."

"Yes. Well, we are not talking about honey."

"I am." Pooh rubbed his tummy. "In fact, I was looking for some but I found you instead."

"We are talking about management."

"I'd rather talk about honey. Before you came along, I thought I heard a buzzing-noise. Why don't we walk down to the old hollow tree and see if the buzzing-noise came from some bees that just might be making honey?"

"We can go down there later, but first I want to talk

about management because it's a Very Important Subject and I think you can help me, if you will."

Pooh cast a lingering look in the direction of the bees that were making the buzzing-noise and then brightened. "If it's a Very Important Subject, and I help you with it, then I might have a chance to become a Very Important Bear."

"That's quite possible. Shall we sit down and talk about it?"

"Bother! I'd really like some honey, but I suppose, that if I want to become a V.I.B., I shall have to." Pooh carefully selected a comfortable-looking stone that had an unobstructed view of the old hollow bee-tree and sat down. "We can talk and at the same time keep an eye on the tree just in case anyone else heard a buzzing-noise and decided to come to see if it came from some bees that might be making honey."

"All right. Now, the reason that management is a Very Important Subject is that if we didn't have management, most important things wouldn't get done, or if they did, they wouldn't get done very well."

"Like going to visit Rabbit and his not having remembered to stock his larder with a pot of honey to put on the bread that he should serve to guests who just happen to drop by and might like to have a mouthful of something?"

"Exactly. That and many other important things."

Pooh sat up straight, taking more of an interest in

the subject of management. "So why don't people who management—"

"—people who manage—"

"—manage learn how to do it properly?"

"That's the problem. Just about everybody agrees on what management is. 'The art and science of directing effort and resources so that the established objectives of an enterprise may be attained in accordance with accepted policies' is one definition. It is the 'How' that nobody is quite sure about."

Pooh nodded, assuming his wise-bear look. "*How* is difficult," he said. "If you ask Eeyore how he is, he almost always says, 'Not very how.' Everyone has trouble with 'How.' I remember once when I heard a buzzing-noise from the top of a tree and decided that there might be honey there. I also decided that I would like to eat a little honey. It was the 'How' to get the honey that was troublesome."

"Well, it is the same thing with management. It seems that almost everyone has a theory about good management and how it can be achieved. There are stacks and stacks of books on the subject. There are books on Theory X and Theory Y and I think even on Theory Z. There are books called *Eupsychian Management* by Abraham Maslow; *The Practice of Management* by Peter Drucker; *Creative Management* by Shigeru Kobayashi; *In Search of Excellence* by Thomas J. Peters and Robert H. Waterman Jr.; *The One-Minute Manager* by Kenneth Blanchard and Spencer Johnson; and on and on and on. They are good books, but—"

"—but they sound very complicated," said Pooh.

"That is why I came to you. Over the past twenty years or so, I think that many managers have been distracted by the theories in these books and by management fads. They have paid too much attention to trying the latest management theory and not enough attention to the real basics of managing. I think that most would improve their performance tremendously by concentrating on these basics of a manager's job.

"I think that many of your adventures illustrate those basic functions of a manager that, if practiced consistently and properly, would help any manager do a really excellent job."

"They would?" Pooh sounded surprised. "Oh, yes. They would," he said in a barely certain kind of voice.

"For instance, the adventure you mentioned—when you tried to get honey—could be used as a good example of the six basic functions in the work of a manager. Those are the things that are common to all managers and what makes them managers rather than something else."

"You mean a manager instead of—say—a bee?" Pooh stared off in the direction of a tree. "I thought I heard a buzzing-sound just then."

The Stranger listened carefully. "I think someone in the village on the far side of the Forest is running a stick along a picket fence."

"Oh. I thought it might have been a bee."

"No. I think it just sounded like a bee."

"I see." Then to show that he had been paying attention, Pooh asked, "What are the six functions of a manager's job?"

"Let's use your adventure of getting the honey to identify them," suggested The Stranger. He opened the picnic basket, took out a little morning snack of something that he kindly gave to Pooh, and then took out a book, which he leafed through until he found the place he wanted. "I believe it went like this." The Stranger began to read.

> One day when he was out walking, he came to an open place in the middle of the forest, and in the middle of this place was a large oak-tree, and, from the top of the tree, there came a loud buzzing-noise.
>
> Winnie-the-Pooh sat down at the foot of the tree, put his head between his paws and began to think.
>
> First of all he said to himself: "That buzzing-noise

means something. You don't get a buzzing-noise like that, just buzzing and buzzing, without its meaning something. If there's a buzzing-noise, somebody's making a buzzing-noise, and the only reason for making a buzzing-noise that I know of is because you're a bee."

Then he thought another long time, and said:

"And the only reason for being a bee that I know of is making honey."

And then he got up, and said: "And the only reason for making honey is so as I can eat it." So he began to climb the tree. . . .

Then as he climbed a little further . . . and a little further . . . and then just a little further. . . .

He was getting rather tired by this time, so that is why he sang a Complaining Song. He was nearly there now, and if he just stood on that branch . . .

Crack! . . .

"It all comes, I suppose," he decided, as he said good-bye to the last branch, spun round three times, and flew gracefully into a gorse-bush, "it all comes of *liking* honey so much. Oh, help!"

He crawled out of the gorse-bush, brushed the prickles from his nose, and began to think again. And the first person he thought of was Christopher Robin. . . .

So Winnie-the-Pooh went round to his friend Christopher Robin, who lived behind a green door in another part of the forest.

"Good morning, Christopher Robin," he said.

"Now, that illustrates the first function a manager should perform, which is Establishing Objectives," said

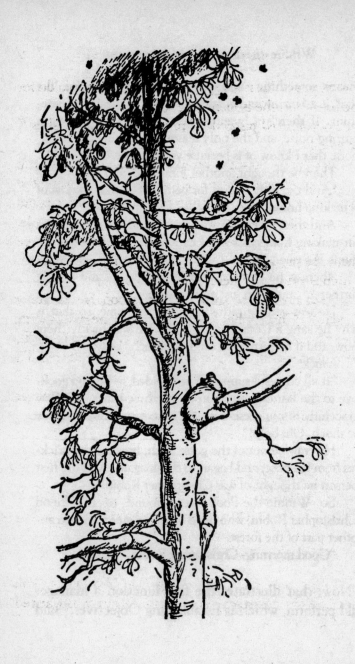

The Stranger. "It is also the first thing she should do for the operation she is managing."

Pooh looked puzzled. "Are managers always 'shes'?" he asked.

"No," The Stranger answered. "Many are hes. You see, pronouns are difficult. The convention of using the male pronoun when referring to a situation that could involve either is confusing and annoys some people. Therefore, when I'm writing or talking, I sometimes use the male pronoun and sometimes the female pronoun, which is what I did here."

Pooh nodded, to show he understood, but he really didn't. "If Christopher Robin were here, he would write the first function with a stick here in this patch of earth, because it sounds like something to be remembered. I'd do it, but he is the only one in the Forest who can spell."

"A good idea. I'll do it as we talk." The Stranger picked up a stick and wrote in the dirt in big letters.

THE SIX FUNCTIONS IN THE WORK OF A MANAGER

1. ESTABLISHING OBJECTIVES

"This was the first thing you did when you noticed the bee-tree. You decided that you wanted to get the honey, and how much of it you wanted."

"All of it," said Pooh wistfully.

"You then went to Christopher Robin whose help was needed to attain the goal and meet the objective." The Stranger continued to read:

> "I wonder if you've got such a thing as a balloon about you?"
>
> "A balloon?"
>
> "Yes, I just said to myself coming along: 'I wonder if Christopher Robin has such a thing as a balloon about him?' I just said it to myself, thinking of balloons, and wondering."
>
> "What do you want a balloon for?" you said.
>
> Winnie-the-Pooh looked round to see that nobody was listening, put his paw to his mouth, and said in a deep whisper: "*Honey!*"
>
> "But you don't get honey with balloons!"
>
> "I do," said Pooh. . . .

Well, you both went out with the blue balloon, and you took your gun with you, just in case, as you always did, and Winnie-the-Pooh went to a very muddy place that he knew of, and rolled and rolled until he was black all over; and then, when the balloon was blown up as big as big, and you and Pooh were both holding on to the string, you let go suddenly, and Pooh Bear floated gracefully up into the sky, and stayed there—level with the top of the tree and about twenty feet away from it.

"That was very good, Pooh," said The Stranger. "You effectively carried out the second function that a good manager performs." Under the first function The Stranger wrote:

2. ORGANIZING

"You analyzed what had to be done in order to reach the objectives. You determined what resources you would need, what jobs needed to be performed, and who would be best suited to do the required work. You made that assignment based on your evaluation of their talents and abilities."

"Christopher Robin had a balloon and a gun just in case something should go wrong and they were needed."

"Exactly. He was best because Rabbit, or Piglet, or Eeyore didn't have those things. Once you had picked Christopher Robin, you went on to the third function, which is Motivating." The Stranger wrote that down as number three.

3. MOTIVATING

"What's moti—motiva—whatever?" asked Pooh.

"Motivating. It means the reason why someone would want to do something. If you, as a manager, want someone to do a job or to help you accomplish an objective, you must find a reason why he or she should help and tell him or her what it is."

"I told Christopher Robin about the honey."

"Since you knew he liked honey, that gave him a reason or a motive to help you get it. He knew that if he helped, he would share it when you achieved your objective. You were motivating him to help you."

"Almost everybody likes Honey," said Pooh. "But it seems to me that there might be another reason. Christopher Robin is always willing to do something to help me, even if there is no honey. I think it's because I'm his favorite bear."

"Excellent," The Stranger complimented him. "Liking someone else can be the strongest motivator of all. That was very astute of you."

"That Kind of Bear!" thought Pooh, although he didn't say it out loud. "What is the fourth function?" he asked instead.

"Developing people. A good manager must make certain to do this, although it is easy to neglect." The Stranger wrote it down.

4. DEVELOPING PEOPLE

"That was what you were doing when you were being a cloud and you were coaching Christopher Robin in how he should act to make the bees think that you were a cloud and not a bear hanging from a balloon. You remember, it went like this."

"Christopher Robin!"
"Yes?"
"Have you an umbrella in your house?"
"I think so."
"I wish you would bring it out here, and walk up and down with it, and look up at me every now and then, and say 'Tut-tut, it looks like rain.' I think, if you did that, it would help the deception which we are practising on these bees."

Well, you laughed to yourself, "Silly old Bear!" but you didn't say it aloud because you were so fond of him, and you went home for your umbrella.

"Oh, there you are!" called down Winnie-the-Pooh, as soon as you got back to the tree. "I was beginning to get anxious. I have discovered that the bees are now definitely Suspicious."

"Shall I put my umbrella up?" you said.

"Yes, but wait a moment. We must be practical. The important bee to deceive is the Queen Bee. Can you see which is the Queen Bee from down there?"

"No."

"A pity. Well, now, if you walk up and down with your umbrella, saying, 'Tut-tut, it looks like rain,' I shall do what I can by singing a little Cloud Song, such as a cloud might sing. . . . Go!"

So, while you walked up and down and wondered if it would rain, Winnie-the-Pooh sang this song:

> *How sweet to be a Cloud*
> *Floating in the Blue!*
> *Every little cloud*
> *Always sings aloud.*
>
> *"How sweet to be a Cloud*
> *Floating in the Blue!"*
> *It makes him very proud*
> *To be a little cloud.*

"You mean when he had put his umbrella up and was walking up and down, and I told him he should say 'Tut, tut, tut, it looks like rain'?"

"Exactly. You were developing his acting ability. What is more, you developed your own 'cloudness' by singing a little Cloud Song."

"Yes." Pooh nodded. "I thought it was one of my better Cloud Songs, but I'm not sure that the bees thought so."

"Well, improvement in performance usually comes in stages. Perhaps next time they will think so. Now here is a great example of the fifth function." The Stranger read from the book.

> "Christopher Robin!" he said in a loud whisper.
> "Hallo!"
> "I think the bees *suspect* something!"
> "What sort of thing?"
> "I don't know. But something tells me that they're *suspicious*!"
> "Perhaps they think that you're after their honey."
> "It may be that. You never can tell with bees." . . .
> The bees were still buzzing as suspiciously as ever. Some of them, indeed, left their nest and flew all round the cloud as it began the second verse of this song, and one bee sat down on the nose of the cloud for a moment, and then got up again.
> "Christopher—*ow!*—Robin," called out the cloud.
> "Yes?"

"I have just been thinking, and I have come to a very important decision. *These are the wrong sort of bees.*"

The Stranger wrote down COMMUNICATING as number five.

5. COMMUNICATING

"Communicating is just telling everyone who has something to do with your project what is going on," said The Stranger. "It's something that happens when you tell them things, and also it has to do with the way you act and work with them."

"Like telling Christopher Robin that the bees were definitely suspicious."

"Yes, and you were also communicating when you said '*ow!*' when the bee stung the nose of the cloud."

"That wasn't meant to be communication," said Pooh, remembering and rubbing the nose of the cloud.

"Nevertheless, it was effective and gave a member of your team information about the true state of the situation, which is what communication is supposed to do."

"That's nice to know. At the time it wasn't so nice."

"I can imagine. Now, the sixth thing that a manager must do is to establish measures of how things are, both in terms of progress toward the objective and in how each individual is doing—her performance, in other words.

"That is called Measurement and Analysis. Remember, you did it this way":

"Christopher Robin, you must shoot the balloon with your gun. Have you got your gun?"

"Of course I have," you said. "But if I do that, it will spoil the balloon," you said.

"But if you *don't*," said Pooh, "I shall have to let go, and that would spoil *me*."

When you put it like this, you saw how it was, and you aimed very carefully at the balloon, and fired.

"*Ow!*" said Pooh.

"Did I miss?" you asked.

"You didn't exactly *miss*," said Pooh, "but you missed the *balloon*."

"I'm so sorry," you said, and you fired again, and this time you hit the balloon, and the air came slowly out, and Winnie-the-Pooh floated down to the ground.

The Stranger wrote:

6. MEASUREMENT AND ANALYSIS

"This is possibly one of the most important factors, because unless individuals know how they are doing and what they are doing correctly, they can't improve their performance. Of course, the results of your measurement must be communicated to everyone on the team.

"You were doing exactly this, Pooh, when you told Christopher Robin that his first shot had missed the balloon. And by telling him what his first shot hit, you enabled him to correct his aim and improve his performance with his second shot."

"I'm glad I did that," said Pooh. "I think."

"Managers are always glad when someone on their team improves their performance."

Pooh was not so certain that he would improve his performance the next time he tried to get honey from the bee-tree unless he did something very different. He climbed down from his rock, walked over, and stood looking at the list of the six functions in the work of a manager to see if they gave him any ideas on how to get the honey that he was almost certain was in the tree where he could hear the buzzing-noise.

THE SIX FUNCTIONS IN THE WORK OF A MANAGER

1. **ESTABLISHING OBJECTIVES**
2. **ORGANIZING**
3. **MOTIVATING**
4. **DEVELOPING PEOPLE**
5. **COMMUNICATING**
6. **MEASUREMENT AND ANALYSIS**

Except they didn't quite look like that because in getting to where he could see them, he had walked across them, so they looked more like this:

1.   ABLISH   OBJECTIVES
2. ORG   ZING
3. MOTI   ING
4. DEVELOP   OPLE
5. COMMUNI   ING
6. MEASUR   ENT AND ANALYSIS

Pooh stood looking down for a while. Finally he said, "What's an 'ENT' that a manager's supposed to measure?"

"It's supposed to be 'MEASUREMENT.' You walked across the list and scuffed out some of the letters."

"Oh. I didn't think we had talked about anything like an 'ENT.' To tell the truth, I was also wondering a little about 'OPLE.' Now I see. But there is one other thing that I don't understand."

"What's that?"

Pooh pointed at the list. "These all look like 'Whats.' It's the 'Hows' that I have trouble with."

"That's very true. However, before we could work on the 'Hows,' we first had to know what the 'Whats' were that the 'Hows' would apply to."

"I see," said Pooh in a puzzled tone of voice that sounded as if he really weren't sure. "Shall we start on the 'Hows'?"

The Stranger looked up at the sun. "It seems to me that it's well past lunchtime. I think we've talked enough for one day. Shall we go down and see if that really was a buzzing-noise made by bees making honey, or would you rather go back to where I left a picnic basket, which I happen to know has a large pot of honey inside it?"

II

IN WHICH Pooh Visits Owl in the
Hundred Acre Wood, Has Management
Theories Explained, and Fears He Is
a Bear of No Brain at All

Pooh was puzzled. Actually, he wasn't so much puzzled as he was confuzzled. Confuzzled was almost the longest word that Pooh knew, and he hadn't known that until Christopher Robin had explained that it meant sort of mixed up and baffled.

Pooh had been feeling confuzzled ever since he had talked to The Stranger about management. It had been a Very Nice Conversation and Pooh had particularly liked the way it ended with the very large pot of honey that The Stranger had thoughtfully brought along in the picnic basket.

Pooh had understood very well about what management was and about the six basic functions in the work of a manager, particularly after The Stranger had mentioned that Pooh had scuffed out some of the letters when he had walked around to look at the list The

Stranger had written in the dirt. That part seemed very simple and easy to understand, even for a Bear of Very Little Brain.

Which was what was confuzzling. It all seemed very simple, except the "How" perhaps, but The Stranger had said that stacks and stacks of books had been written about the theories of management and had named some of them. If it seemed simple, why had so many books been written? Perhaps he, Pooh, didn't really understand, after all.

It was a fine spring morning in the forest as he started out. Little soft clouds played happily in a blue sky, skipping from time to time in front of the sun as if they had come to put it out, and then sliding away suddenly so that the next might have his turn. Through them and between them the sun shone bravely; and a copse which had worn its firs all the year round seemed old and dowdy now beside the new green lace which the beeches had put on so prettily. Through copse and spinney marched Bear; down open slopes of gorse and heather, over rocky beds of streams, up steep banks of sandstone into the heather again; and so at last, tired and hungry, to the Hundred Acre Wood. For it was in the Hundred Acre Wood that Owl lived.

"And if anyone knows anything about anything," said Bear to himself, "it's Owl who knows something about something," he said, "or my name's not Winnie-the-Pooh," he said. "Which it is," he added. "So there you are."

Owl lived at The Chestnuts, an old-world residence of great charm, which was grander than anybody else's, or seemed so to Bear, because it had both a knocker *and* a bell-pull. Underneath the knocker there was a notice which said:

PLES RING IF AN RNSER IS REQIRD.

Underneath the bell-pull there was a notice which said:

PLEZ CNOKE IF AN RNSR IS NOT REQID.

These notices had been written by Christopher Robin, who was the only one in the forest who could spell; for Owl, wise though he was in many ways, able to read and write and spell his own name WOL, yet somehow went all to pieces over delicate words like MEASLES and BUTTERED TOAST.

Winnie-the-Pooh read the two notices very carefully, first from left to right, and afterwards, in case he had missed some of it, from right to left. Then, to make quite sure, he knocked and pulled the knocker, and he pulled and knocked the bell-rope, and he called out in a very loud voice, "Owl! I require an answer! It's Bear speaking." And the door opened, and Owl looked out.

"Hallo, Pooh," he said. "How's things?"

"Confuzzled," said Pooh. "And I thought you could help me. About management, that is."

"Well," said Owl. "That's a Very Serious Subject and might take awhile. Could you stay for lunch?"

"I think I could stay that long," said Pooh, trying to see over Owl's shoulder if his larder was as well stocked as usual. "Nothing elaborate though. Just a mouthful of condensed milk or whatnot, with perhaps a lick of honey—unless, of course, you have a pot of honey that is old and just might spoil soon unless somebody who wanted to do a favor finished it off. In which case, I would help—finish it off, that is."

Owl moved out of the door. "Come in then. Just let me put *The Wall Street Journal* I was reading to one side and we can begin."

"With lunch, I hope," said Pooh. "By the way, I see that my friend Eeyore has lost his tail again."

"Eh?" Owl looked out the door. "I don't see Eeyore out there."

"I meant the bell-rope. The last time I saw it Eeyore was attached to it."

Owl peered at the bell-rope. "Oh, yes. Well, I can see why he would be. I'm rather fond of it myself. It lends a certain air of distinction to my entrance. Actually, it looks remarkably like the one I had previously. Someone unhooked it and took it away just after you visited here that time you were looking for Eeyore's tail. I found this one in the Forest on a bush, just like the last one. It must be that someone is manufacturing them and then being careless when they go through the Forest to market."

"Oh," said Pooh. "I hadn't thought of that."

"Yes. Well, let's sit down and get started."

"With lunch," said Pooh quickly. "Or perhaps we could start with elevenses," he said, glancing at the clock ticking away on Owl's mantelpiece. "I generally have a little something at eleven o'clock in the morning, and it's almost that now."

"Why, so it is," said Owl. "I generally have something myself."

"And then we could have lunch later."

After they had both had a little something, and then had lunch, Owl and Pooh settled down on either side of the fireplace. It was getting blusterous outside, but Owl's house was well constructed, and the fire danced and crackled and threw off a nice warm glow.

Pooh felt that this was a very good place to learn about management theory.

"Well, Pooh," said Owl. "Where shall we start?"

"I don't know," said Pooh. "Since I don't know anything about management theory—except," he said hastily, lest Owl think he was a Bear of Very Little Brain, "what somebody does that makes him a manager instead of, say, a bee—or something else."

"I wasn't asking you the question," said Owl. "I was asking myself."

"I thought you were asking me. I distinctly heard you say, 'Well, Pooh, where shall we start?' "

"That was just a manner of speaking, like when you say to Piglet, 'Isn't it a beautiful day?' You don't really expect an answer because he can see it is a beautiful day."

"Oh," said Pooh. "I see."

"Good," said Owl, relieved that that had been cleared up. "Now, where shall we begin?"

Forgetting that Owl was probably asking himself the question, Pooh said, "I've always found that a good place to begin is at the beginning, because otherwise things can get very confuzzled. If you begin at the end, it's not very interesting, because you already know how things ended before you begin, and if you begin at the middle, you can't go both ways at the same time, and—"

"We will," pronounced Owl firmly, "begin at the beginning."

"Good," said Pooh, and scrunched back in his chair
to be in the proper listening position and to get more
comfortable.

"One of the earliest records we have about management theory," continued Owl, "is in the eighteenth
chapter of Exodus in the Bible. Moses was the leader of
a tribe of people called the Israelites."

Owl paused and peered at Pooh. "As you know, it is
desirable that a manager be a leader." Pooh nodded to
show that he knew that, although he hadn't, really. Not
until Owl said it.

"Anyway, Moses was having trouble doing a good
job because he was trying to do everything. His father-
in-law, Jethro, seeing what was happening, told Moses
to pick out some good people and let them handle
some of the less important work. This would give
Moses more time to do the really important parts of his
job. Doing that is called 'Delegation,' and it is a very
Important and Necessary thing for a manager to do,
even today."

Pooh said "Del-e-ga-tion" to himself several times
so that he would remember to ask The Stranger about
where it fit into the six functions of a manager's job. It
sounded as if it just might be a "How."

He also made up a little Manager Song so he would
remember to ask The Stranger about a leader.

The manager, manager,
A leader should be.
That's Most Important,
As we all can see.

He hummed it under his breath until Owl looked at him and asked him if the lunch had not agreed with him because he was making a strange sound.

Pooh said that he was fine and it was a very good lunch, indeed. The sound was just a sound he made when he was trying to remember something.

"Good," said Owl. "Now, the Exodus happened a long time ago, but, ever since then, people have thought about management and have been writing about it."

"That's what The Stranger said. He said there were books about Theory X and Theory Y and Theory Z and lots of others that I forget right now."

And then Pooh had to stop and tell Owl about The Stranger and what he had said. After he had finished, Owl nodded wisely.

"I think we can skip over a lot of the in-between things about management and talk about the more recent theories, like X and Y."

"Good," said Pooh. He rather liked the idea of Theory X because "X" was one of the letters that he knew he could make. You just took two sticks that were the same size and put one on top of the other so that their middles touched.

You had to be careful how you did it, because you might get something that Christopher Robin said was a PLUS sign, which meant something completely different from "X."

Pooh also liked "X" because it was the first letter of a lot of words that meant good things, like Xcellent, Xciting, Xceptional (the kind of Bear Christopher Robin said that he was), and Xtremely delicious, like honey.

Sometimes, when nobody was around, Pooh would make an "X" when he found two of the right-size sticks in the Forest, just to remind himself about "X."

"X and Y," Owl went on, "were what Douglas Mc-Gregor, in his book, *The Human Side of Enterprise*, called the two basic choices for managing the worker and working.

"Theory X was the traditional approach, and it assumes that people are lazy and shiftless, work only because they have no choice, dislike working, and have to be driven. It also assumes that people can't take responsibility for themselves and their actions and have to be looked after.

"Theory Y, on the other hand—"

"Why is it on the other hand?" interrupted Pooh.

"What! What?" asked Owl.

"Why is Theory Y on the other hand? I didn't know that Theory X was on the first hand."

"Oh, I see," said Owl. "That is just a way of saying

'as distinguished from' the first thing we were talking about."

"I see," said Pooh, although he didn't. This management theory was difficult to understand sometimes.

"As I was saying, before I was interrupted"—Owl peered sternly at Pooh—"Theory Y assumes that people have a need to work and that they want to do things and take responsibility. They don't want somebody to take care of them. They want to do it themselves.

"As you can see, Pooh, the two theories are exactly opposite. The question is, which one is right? McGregor, who wrote the book, pretended to be impartial, but there was little question that he felt that Theory Y was the way to manage work and workers."

Owl peered at Pooh. "Which one do you think is right?" he asked.

Pooh thought about the two theories until he was sure he had them straight in his mind. Then he thought about all the things he and his friends had done that needed managing. Then he thought about all his friends and everyone he knew. Then he thought about himself.

He thought so long and so hard that he finally thought that he probably needed Strengthening, which he just happened to mention to Owl.

Owl said it was almost teatime anyway, and although he didn't have any of Roo's Strengthening Medicine, perhaps a little more condensed milk and honey on bread might serve the purpose.

"That is possible," said Pooh. "Anyway, it is worth trying."

So they each had a little something, although Pooh's little something was a little more than Owl's little something. Still, when he had licked off the last little bit of honey from the plate, Pooh did feel considerably strengthened.

While Owl cleaned up the dishes and poked up the fire, because it was getting chilly and late in the day, Pooh thought some more.

Finally he shook his head. "I fear I am a Bear of No Brain at All! I can't decide which one is right and which one is wrong. The theories are exactly the opposite; if one is right, then the other must be wrong. It seems to me that some, like Eeyore, would be happier with Theory X and others, like Rabbit, would like Theory Y better. As for myself, sometimes I need taking care of and sometimes I don't. If someone needed taking care of, then Theory Y would not be at all Nice for them."

"Congratulations, Pooh," said Owl. "That is exactly the conclusion that Abraham H. Maslow came to in his book, *Eupsychian Management*. Peter Drucker, who is recognized as an expert in management, concluded that the question is not which theory is right, but that each manager must decide what is right for her own situation. He also said that a new theory is needed because neither Theory X nor Theory Y seem to work very well in all organizations.

"So you see, Pooh, you are not a Bear of No Brain at All. You came to the same conclusion as did some very smart people who are experts in management."

THAT sort of Bear! thought Pooh, feeling much better although still a little confuzzled. He stood up. "Thank you, Owl, for explaining things to me. I had better be leaving now because it is getting late, and it seems to be more blusterous outside than it was."

"Any time at all, Pooh," said Owl as he opened the door. "It is always a pleasure to discuss Very Serious Subjects."

It was very blusterous indeed, and besides he had a feeling that it must be getting close to supper time, so Pooh hurried toward home, jumping down the banks of creeks and bending over to miss low-hanging branches instead of going around.

Still, when he saw the Old Grey Donkey, Eeyore, standing in a thistly corner of the Forest, he thought about the bell-pull at Owl's, slowed down, and went over to him.

"And how are you?" said Winnie-the-Pooh.
Eeyore shook his head from side to side.

"Not very how," he said. "I don't seem to have felt at all how for a long time."

"Dear, dear," said Pooh, "I'm sorry about that. Let's have a look at you."

So Eeyore stood there, gazing sadly at the ground, and Winnie-the-Pooh walked all round him once.

"Why, what's happened to your tail?" he said in surprise.

"What *has* happened to it?" said Eeyore.

"It isn't there!"

"Are you sure?"

"Well, either a tail *is* there or it isn't there. You can't make a mistake about it. And yours *isn't* there!"

"Then what is?"

"Nothing."

"Let's have a look," said Eeyore, and he turned slowly round to the place where his tail had been a little while ago, and then, finding that he couldn't catch it up, he turned round the other way, until he came back to where he was at first, and then he put his head down and looked between his front legs, and at last he said, with a long, sad sigh, "I believe you're right."

"Of course I'm right," said Pooh.

"How like it not to be there," said Eeyore gloomily. "It wasn't there once before, you know."

"Yes, but I think I know where it is, this time. It's at Owl's pretending to be a bell-rope."

"How Strange," said Eeyore. "Some are never satisfied to be What They Are but always want to be Something Else."

"If you go to Owl and ask him, he probably would give it back to you since he has a knocker already. But be sure to ask him nicely, because he said he was fond of it."

"I could tell him that I was attached to it," said Eeyore. "That might convince him, but I doubt it. Oh, well, I might as well try. Thank you, Pooh."

And Eeyore set off in the direction of Owl's house.

"Well," said Pooh to himself, since Eeyore had already left, "at least I think I was right that there are some people who need to be taken care of, sometimes."

III

In which The Stranger, Pooh, and Rabbit Talk About the "Hows" of Setting Objectives and Organizing and Pooh Forgets to Sing His Manager Song

Sometimes Pooh thought that Rabbit was almost as Bouncy as Tigger. At other times, he thought that in Bounciness, nobody could quite come up to Tigger. Not Rabbit. Not even Kanga. The thing was, Kanga's and Rabbit's Bounciness was a controlled sort of Bounce, whereas there was no telling just where Tigger's Bounce would land him.

So Pooh was glad it was Rabbit and not Tigger who came Bouncing along while he was waiting for The Stranger.

Sometimes Tigger forgot that he had been un-Bounced, and that might put The Stranger off if he wasn't expecting to be Bounced on.

"Hallo, Rabbit," said Pooh.

"Good morning, Pooh," said Rabbit. "What are you doing?"

"Thinking about being a V.I.B. and waiting for The Stranger." And then Pooh had to explain about The Stranger and management and the chance to become a Very Important Bear and everything.

"I see," said Rabbit, when Pooh had finished. "That sounds very interesting."

"Why don't you stay?" asked Pooh. He remembered that Rabbit was one of the smarter and more educated ones in the Forest, and it might be nice for The Stranger to have him there. He also remembered about Motivation and quickly mentioned that The Stranger had had some Very Fine Looking snacks in his picnic basket last time.

"That's not to say that it is certain that he will bring along another picnic basket today, but since he did before, he just might again and very kindly offer to share."

Rabbit didn't have to answer the question, because

just then The Stranger came along through the Forest carrying a picnic basket. Pooh made the introductions and The Stranger and Rabbit said the kind of things that everyone says when they are being introduced. When it was all done, it seemed to be taken for granted that Rabbit would stay.

Then, of course, Pooh had to tell The Stranger about his conversation with Owl about management theory.

"It sounds to me as if Owl did a very good job telling you about those management theories," The Stranger said when Pooh had finished. "I also think that your comments were addressing the really important issue, that of differences. You are very insightful, Pooh."

At that, Pooh felt very good, and he even stopped wondering if there was another pot of honey in the picnic basket that The Stranger had brought.

"You see, if we stop to think about it, we all know that the same individual will react differently under different circumstances and conditions. We also know that each of us is different in our nature, in what we like and don't like, and in our outlook on life and what we want to get from it."

"Rabbit likes to have bread and condensed milk with his honey, but I don't mind just honey," said Pooh, · looking at the picnic basket. "I just thought I'd mention that as an example."

"That's a good example. If I had a job that needed

doing and I needed the help of you both, if I offered only fish and chips as a reason for helping, then neither of you might be very interested. Which reminds me, I just happen to have some bread and condensed milk and a pot of honey in my picnic basket, which are more than I can eat. I would really appreciate it if you could both help me when it is time for lunch so that it doesn't spoil."

Pooh and Rabbit both agreed that they would be willing to do that, just so it wouldn't go to waste.

"So," The Stranger continued, "it is difficult to set up one kind of management organization that will work perfectly for everyone. As Peter Drucker says in his book, *Management: Tasks, Responsibilities, Practices,* 'We do not yet have a genuine theory of business and no integrated discipline of business management.' "

"It seems to me then," said Rabbit, who had been listening very carefully, "if that is the case, it makes the manager's job a difficult one."

"It does. But still, it is the manager's responsibility to meet her objectives, so she has to do the best with what she has. She must decide what the reality of her situation is and work with that."

"If Eeyore was here," said Pooh, "he would say that is Discouraging and Sad."

"Not totally. We can look at companies and organizations like Procter & Gamble, 3M, Microsoft, and others that have done a very good job over the years by looking clearly at reality and structuring the way they operate so that they and most of their people perform very well, in spite of there not being an adequate management theory available to them."

"But what about the manager who doesn't work for one of those organizations?" asked Rabbit. "What is he to do?"

"I think the most important thing he can do is to pay regular and careful attention to doing the very best job he possibly can on carrying out the six basic functions of a manager," said The Stranger.

"You see, in this area, the manager has almost complete control of how and what he does. He might not be able, for instance, to have his company change over to a system like 3M's, and indeed it might not be practical or even possible, but he can improve his own performance as a manager.

"In addition, although our knowledge about human nature and management theory is inadequate, we do know quite a bit about the six functions of a manager's job."

"It's the 'Hows' that are difficult," said Pooh.

"Well," said The Stranger, "why don't we take one of your adventures and look at it and see what sort of 'Hows' we can find about the first two basic functions: Establishing Objectives and Organizing."

"Good," said Pooh. "I always like to start at the beginning."

"Since Rabbit is here, what about using an adventure that the two of you shared? Can you think of one that had establishing objectives and organizing as part of it?"

"What about the time Kanga and Baby Roo came to the Forest?" asked Rabbit.

"That might be a very good choice," said The Stranger thoughtfully. "Now, let me see, how did that start?"

Nobody seemed to know where they came from, but there they were in the Forest: Kanga and Baby Roo. When Pooh asked Christopher Robin, "How did they come here?" Christopher Robin said, "In the Usual Way, if you know what I mean, Pooh," and Pooh, who didn't, said "Oh!" Then he nodded his head twice and said, "In the Usual Way. Ah!" Then he went to call upon his friend Piglet to see what *he* thought about it. And at Piglet's house he found Rabbit. So they all talked about it together.

"What I don't like about it is this," said Rabbit.

"Here are we—you, Pooh, and you, Piglet, and Me—and suddenly—"

"And Eeyore," said Pooh.

"And Eeyore—and then suddenly—"

"And Owl," said Pooh.

"And Owl—and then all of a sudden—"

"Oh, and Eeyore," said Pooh. "I was forgetting *him*."

"Here—we—are," said Rabbit very slowly and carefully, "all—of—us, and then, suddenly, we wake up one morning and, what do we find? We find a Strange Animal among us. An animal of whom we have never even heard before! An animal who carries her family about with her in her pocket! Suppose *I* carried *my* family about with me in *my* pocket, how many pockets should I want?"

"Sixteen," said Piglet.

"Seventeen, isn't it?" said Rabbit. "And one more for a handkerchief—that's eighteen. Eighteen pockets in one suit! I haven't time."

There was a long and thoughtful silence ... and then Pooh, who had been frowning very hard for some minutes, said: "I make it fifteen."

"What?" said Rabbit.

"Fifteen."

"Fifteen what?"

"Your family."

"What about them?"

Pooh rubbed his nose and said that he thought Rabbit had been talking about his family.

"Did I?" said Rabbit carelessly.

"Yes, you said—"

"Never mind, Pooh," said Piglet impatiently.

"The question is, What are we to do about Kanga?"

"Oh, I see," said Pooh.

"The best way," said Rabbit, "would be this. The best way would be to steal Baby Roo and hide him, and then when Kanga says, 'Where's Baby Roo?' we say, '*Aha!*' "

"*Aha!*" said Pooh, practising. "*Aha! Aha!* ... Of course," he went on, "we could say '*Aha!*' even if we hadn't stolen Baby Roo."

"Pooh," said Rabbit kindly, "you haven't any brain."

"I know," said Pooh humbly.

"We say '*Aha!*' so that Kanga knows that *we* know where Baby Roo is. '*Aha!*' means 'We'll tell you where Baby Roo is, if you promise to go away from the Forest and never come back.' Now don't talk while I think."

"That was what we decided at the time," said Pooh. "If we had to decide it now, I think we would decide differently, because Kanga is really very nice and not at all Strange."

"That is only because we have gotten to know Kanga," said Rabbit. "If you take the time to get to know someone, you usually find they are not so strange after all, even if they seem very different at first. But we are not talking about NOW. We are talking about THEN. At the time Kanga seemed like a Strange Animal that we would be better off not having in the Forest."

The Stranger had been listening carefully to all of

this because he had forgotten some things about the story.

"If I understand it correctly, then," he said, "the objective that you established was to get Kanga to leave the Forest and never come back."

"Yes," said Rabbit.

"Yesssss," said Pooh in an I'm-not-quite-sure tone of voice. "But we also decided to steal Baby Roo and hide him and not give him back unless Kanga left the Forest. Isn't that an objective?"

"Well, let's see," said The Stranger. "When a manager is setting objectives in her area of responsibility, those objectives should follow certain rules. Those rules tell us 'How' to set objectives that are valid and appropriate. If we review those rules, maybe we can decide what your objective really was and if you did a good job in establishing it."

"I like learning about the 'How,'" said Pooh. "'Hows' are difficult."

"The first rule for establishing objectives is that they must be derived from and be in accordance with the basic purpose or mission of the organization. In other words, you have to know what the organization was set up to do, what its business really is. Then you can design your objectives in any particular situation so they will make a contribution to accomplishing that purpose.

"Without a clear understanding of what the organization's mission is, there is no way a manager can decide what his objectives should be."

"Who decides what the purpose of an organization is?" asked Rabbit.

"That is one of the primary responsibilities of top management. Unfortunately, it also is one that is frequently neglected. Often everyone thinks that the answer is obvious. Usually it isn't, and determining it requires a lot of hard work and thinking. When top management hasn't established what the purpose is, the organization will almost always get into trouble.

"A good example of this is railroads in the United States. Everyone connected with them knew that their business was 'railroading.' Actually, the purpose of their business was to move or transport things from one place to another. They concentrated on railroading while the trucking companies and airlines took away their business. By not establishing what their purpose or mission was, the railroads missed opportunities and came on hard times.

"They had confused the means, a railroad, with the ends—viable and appropriate transportation."

"I can understand that," said Pooh. "Maybe stealing Baby Roo was a means and not an objective."

"I think it may be too soon to decide until we know the other rules," said The Stranger. "Let's go on and cover those.

"The second rule comes from the fact that you can't

do an objective or a goal. The objective must be able to be translated into specific work and assignments that will be carried out to reach the goal.

"Next, the objective must concentrate on the really important things so that you make the best use of the resources available to you since no one and no organization has all the resources needed to do everything.

"Then you should always have multiple objectives, because in any endeavor you are trying to balance a variety of needs, and that requires more than one objective.

"Objectives must make sense. The questions you ask to determine this are: 'Is it reasonable?' and 'Can we do it?'

"If the answer you get is no, then you had better redraft your objectives. Few individuals will work very well to achieve something when they perceive that failure is preordained.

"Finally, objectives should not be cast in concrete, since they are based on a guess about the future— ideally, an informed guess, but still a guess. Since the future holds many surprises and many conditions are beyond our control, objectives should recognize this fact and contain an allowance for it."

"It seems to me," said Rabbit slowly, "that we didn't do badly in setting our objectives according to the rules except we should have paid more attention to the purpose of our organization before we set our objectives.

Then we should have had more of an allowance for things not going as we expected."

"Why is that?" asked The Stranger.

"I know," said Pooh. "If we had spent more time talking about our purpose, we might have seen that we felt that Kanga and Baby Roo coming to the Forest was possibly a threat to us. The purpose of our organization then would be to see if it really was a threat, and if so, what we should do about it."

"We just hopped to a conclusion," said Rabbit, "that Kanga was a threat, so that limited us in choosing our objectives."

"That's the trouble with not knowing what the real purpose or mission of an organization is," said The Stranger.

"Yes," said Pooh. "We could have had an objective of finding out if Kanga was a threat, say, by asking Christopher Robin."

"Or," added Rabbit, "by sending Piglet to say 'Hallo' to Kanga while Pooh and I watched to see if she ate him—"

"Which Piglet wouldn't have liked. But either plan would have been easier than what we did do," finished Pooh.

"What happened then?" asked The Stranger.

"Piglet had an objection," said Pooh, remembering.

"There's just one thing," said Piglet, fidgeting a bit. "I was talking to Christopher Robin, and he said that a

Kanga was Generally Regarded as One of the Fiercer Animals. I am not frightened of Fierce Animals in the ordinary way, but it is well known that, if One of the Fiercer Animals is Deprived of Its Young, it becomes as fierce as Two of the Fiercer Animals. In which case '*Aha!*' is perhaps a *foolish* thing to say."

"Piglet," said Rabbit, taking out a pencil, and licking the end of it, "you haven't any pluck."

"It is hard to be brave," said Piglet, sniffing slightly, "when you're only a Very Small Animal."

Rabbit, who had begun to write very busily, looked up and said:

"It is because you are a very small animal that you will be Useful in the adventure before us."

Piglet was so excited at the idea of being Useful that he forgot to be frightened any more, and when Rabbit went on to say that Kangas were only Fierce during the winter months, being at other times of an Affectionate Disposition, he could hardly sit still, he was so eager to begin being useful at once.

"What about me?" said Pooh sadly. "I suppose *I* shan't be useful?"

"Never mind, Pooh," said Piglet comfortingly. "Another time perhaps."

"Without Pooh," said Rabbit solemnly as he sharpened his pencil, "the adventure would be impossible."

"Oh!" said Piglet, and tried not to look disappointed. But Pooh went into a corner of the room and said proudly to himself, "Impossible without Me! *That* sort of Bear."

"Now listen all of you," said Rabbit when he had finished writing, and Pooh and Piglet sat listening very eagerly with their mouths open. This was what Rabbit read out:

PLAN TO CAPTURE BABY ROO

1. *General Remarks*. Kanga runs faster than any of Us, even Me.
2. *More General Remarks*. Kanga never takes her eye off Baby Roo, except when he's safely buttoned up in her pocket.
3. *Therefore*. If we are to capture Baby Roo, we must get a Long Start, because Kanga runs faster than any of Us, even Me. (*See* 1.)
4. *A Thought*. If Roo had jumped out of Kanga's pocket and Piglet had jumped in, Kanga wouldn't

know the difference, because Piglet is a Very Small Animal.

5. Like Roo.
6. But Kanga would have to be looking the other way first, so as not to see Piglet jumping in.
7. See 2.
8. *Another Thought*. But if Pooh was talking to her very excitedly, she *might* look the other way for a moment.
9. And then I could run away with Roo.
10. Quickly.
11. *And Kanga wouldn't discover the difference until Afterwards.*

"Then what did you do?" The Stranger asked Rabbit.

"I read it out and answered any questions they had. Then by going over it very carefully, I made certain that they each knew what it was they had to do. I also added into the plan any suggestions and ideas they had."

"I suggested that I tell Kanga a little bit of poetry," said Pooh proudly. "To distract her, you see, which was my part in the Plan."

"I think you did an excellent job of Organizing," said The Stranger.

"I did?" Rabbit sounded surprised. "Oh, yes. I did."

"When a manager organizes, he analyzes the activities and the decisions that are needed to meet the objectives. He develops a step-by-step plan and puts it in writing so that everyone connected with the endeavor can refer to it.

"The plan must tell when each step is to be done and who is responsible for doing it. He then classifies the work and divides it into manageable jobs. According to the requirements of those jobs, he selects individuals whose experience, talents, and abilities match those requirements and assigns them.

"Then he reviews the plan with the individuals, answers their objections, and incorporates their suggestions, when they are appropriate, into the plan.

"He then makes certain that each individual understands the plan and knows what they have to do.

"So, you can see, you did all of those things."

"Yes," said Rabbit. "Considering that we probably started with the wrong purpose, it was a good plan."

"And you did a good job of organizing," said Pooh.

"Thank you, Pooh," said Rabbit. "I couldn't have done it without you."

"I know," said Pooh modestly.

"My goodness," said The Stranger, looking at the sun and noticing that it was almost directly overhead. "It's time for lunch. Why don't we eat and you can tell me how it all came out."

So they opened up the picnic basket, spread a cloth in a nice shady spot, arranged all the food so that it was convenient to reach, and Rabbit began.

"We all went out to look for Kanga and Roo."

Kanga and Roo were spending a quiet afternoon in a sandy part of the Forest. Baby Roo was practising very small jumps in the sand, and falling down mouse-holes and climbing out of them, and Kanga was fidgeting about and saying, "Just one more jump, dear, and then we must go home." And at that moment who should come stumping up the hill but Pooh.

"Good afternoon, Kanga."

"Good afternoon, Pooh."

"Look at me jumping," squeaked Roo, and fell into another mouse-hole.

"Hallo, Roo, my little fellow!"

"We were just going home," said Kanga. "Good afternoon, Rabbit. Good afternoon, Piglet."

Rabbit and Piglet, who had now come up from the

other side of the hill, said, "Good afternoon," and "Hallo, Roo," and Roo asked them to look at him jumping, so they stayed and looked.

And Kanga looked too. . . .

"Oh, Kanga," said Pooh, after Rabbit had winked at him twice, "I don't know if you are interested in Poetry at all?"

"Hardly at all," said Kanga.

"Oh!" said Pooh.

"Roo, dear, just one more jump and then we must go home."

There was a short silence while Roo fell down another mouse-hole.

"Go on," said Rabbit in a loud whisper behind his paw.

"Talking of Poetry," said Pooh, "I made up a little piece as I was coming along. It went like this. Er—now let me see—"

"Fancy!" said Kanga. "Now Roo, dear—"

"You'll like this piece of poetry," said Rabbit.

"You'll love it," said Piglet.

"You must listen very carefully," said Rabbit.

"So as not to miss any of it," said Piglet.

"Oh, yes," said Kanga, but she still looked at Baby Roo.

"*How* did it go, Pooh?" said Rabbit.

Pooh gave a little cough and began.

LINES WRITTEN BY A BEAR
OF VERY LITTLE BRAIN

On Monday, when the sun is hot
I wonder to myself a lot:
"Now is it true, or is it not,

"That what is which and which is what?"
On Tuesday, when it hails and snows,
The feeling on me grows and grows
That hardly anybody knows
If those are these or these are those.

On Wednesday, when the sky is blue,
And I have nothing else to do,
I sometimes wonder if it's true
That who is what and what is who.

On Thursday, when it starts to freeze
And hoar-frost twinkles on the trees,
How very readily one sees
That these are whose—but whose are these?

On Friday—

"Yes, it is, isn't it?" said Kanga, not waiting to hear what happened on Friday. "Just one more jump, Roo, dear, and then we really *must* be going."

Rabbit gave Pooh a hurrying-up sort of nudge.

"Talking of Poetry," said Pooh quickly, "have you ever noticed that tree right over there?"

"Where?" said Kanga. "Now, Roo—"

"That was well done," said The Stranger. "If a manager finds a plan is not working, it should be changed as soon as possible."

"Thank you," said Pooh. "Go ahead Rabbit, read us the rest."

"Right over there," said Pooh, pointing behind Kanga's back.

"No," said Kanga. "Now jump in, Roo, dear, and we'll go home."

"You ought to look at that tree right over there," said Rabbit. "Shall I lift you in, Roo?" And he picked up Roo in his paws.

"I can see a bird in it from here," said Pooh. "Or is it a fish?"

"You ought to see that bird from here," said Rabbit. "Unless it's a fish."

"It isn't a fish, it's a bird," said Piglet.

"So it is," said Rabbit.

"Is it a starling or a blackbird?" said Pooh.

"That's the whole question," said Rabbit. "Is it a blackbird or a starling?"

And then at last Kanga did turn her head to look. And the moment that her head was turned, Rabbit said in a loud voice "In you go, Roo!" and in jumped Piglet into Kanga's pocket, and off scampered Rabbit, with Roo in his paws, as fast as he could.

"Why, where's Rabbit?" said Kanga, turning round again. "Are you all right, Roo, dear?"

Piglet made a squeaky Roo-noise from the bottom of Kanga's pocket.

"Rabbit had to go away," said Pooh. "I think he thought of something he had to go and see about suddenly."

"And Piglet?"

"I think Piglet thought of something at the same time. Suddenly."

"So then the plan worked perfectly," said The Stranger. "Well-l-l-l," said Pooh slowly. "Not exactly."

Of course as soon as Kanga unbuttoned her pocket, she saw what had happened. Just for a moment, she thought she was frightened, and then she knew she wasn't; for she felt quite sure that Christopher Robin would never let any harm happen to Roo. So she said to herself, "If they are having a joke with me, I will have a joke with them."

"Now then, Roo, dear," she said, as she took Piglet out of her pocket. "Bed-time."

"*Aha!*" said Piglet, as well as he could after his Terrifying Journey. But it wasn't a very good "*Aha!*" and Kanga didn't seem to understand what it meant.

"Bath first," said Kanga in a cheerful voice.

"*Aha!*" said Piglet again, looking round anxiously for the others. But the others weren't there. Rabbit was playing with Baby Roo in his own house, and feeling more fond of him every minute, and Pooh, who had decided to be a Kanga, was still at the sandy place on top of the Forest, practising jumps.

"I am not at all sure," said Kanga in a thoughtful voice, "that it wouldn't be a good idea to have a *cold* bath this evening. Would you like that, Roo, dear?"

Piglet, who had never been really fond of baths, shuddered a long indignant shudder, and said in as brave a voice as he could:

"Kanga, I see the time has come to spleak painly."

"Funny little Roo," said Kanga, as she got the bath-water ready.

"I am *not* Roo," said Piglet loudly. "I am Piglet!"

"Yes, dear, yes," said Kanga soothingly. "And imitating Piglet's voice too! So clever of him," she went on, as she took a large bar of yellow soap out of the cupboard. "What *will* he be doing next?"

"Can't you *see?*" shouted Piglet. "Haven't you got *eyes?* Look at me!"

"I *am* looking, Roo, dear," said Kanga rather severely. "And you know what I told you yesterday about making faces. If you go on making faces like Piglet's, you will grow up to *look* like Piglet—and *then* think how sorry you will be. Now then, into the bath, and don't let me have to speak to you about it again."

Before he knew where he was, Piglet was in the bath, and Kanga was scrubbing him firmly with a large lathery flannel.

"She also made him take some of Roo's Strengthening Medicine, which Piglet didn't like in the least, although Kanga told him it really was quite a nice taste when you got used to it." Pooh thought for a moment. "I'm really not quite sure that's true. At least I'm certain that I would never prefer it to honey. Still, I suppose it does make you strong. Look how far Kanga can jump."

"Then Christopher Robin came by and told Kanga that Roo was at my house playing," said Rabbit. "Actually, I became quite fond of him, and we are now great friends."

"And Christopher Robin had left the door open, and Piglet managed to escape and roll on the ground so that he got his own comfortable color back again," Pooh added.

"That was a very exciting adventure," said The Stranger. "Thank you for telling me how it came out."

And then he remembered that he had an appointment outside the Forest, so he quickly packed up his picnic basket and, telling Pooh he would see him tomorrow, left.

"Rabbit," said Pooh. "It seems to me that today is Tuesday."

"Yes," said Rabbit. "And if today is Tuesday, I'm supposed to be playing with Roo."

"And I'm supposed to meet Kanga for my weekly jumping lessons."

So they both hurried off in different directions.

On the way to the sandy place in the Forest, which was the best place to practice jumping, because if you fell down, you didn't hurt yourself, Pooh remembered that he had forgotten to sing his Manager Song for The Stranger.

"Bother," said Pooh. "Oh, well. I'll surely remember to sing it tomorrow—or maybe the next day."

IV

IN WHICH Piglet, Pooh, and Tigger
Communicate After a Fashion, Learn the
Rules, and Pooh Is a Very Forgetful Bear

"It has to be Wednesday," said Pooh.

"Why is that, Pooh?" asked Piglet.

"It just stands to reason. If yesterday was Tuesday, and
tomorrow is Thursday, then today must be Wednesday."

Piglet thought about that for a moment. "Why does
it have to be Wednesday?"

"Because, Piglet," explained Pooh patiently,
"Wednesday always comes after Tuesday and before
Thursday. So it comes in the middle."

"Not always," said Piglet.

"Always," said Pooh, being very firm.

"I remember last year it was Tuesday and then the
next day was Christmas and the following day was
Thursday," said Piglet, even more firmly. "I remember
because it was a Particularly Fine Christmas. It had
snowed very hard on Tuesday, the day before, which is

how I remember it was Tuesday, and I had a Christmas tree which I had Very Carefully Decorated. When I got up on Christmas I found a large gift of haycorns under the tree, and a big red balloon that Christopher Robin had given me—"

"And a pot of honey, which I had given you."

"Which you ate all of, when you came around to wish me a Merry Christmas."

"Yes, I know. There's nothing like a good pot of honey on Christmas morning," said Pooh dreamily. "Or for that matter, anytime."

"But it was my gift, and you ate it all."

"It's the thought that counts," said Pooh.

"Oh," said Piglet. "That's true. I forgot. But, anyway, that proves it."

"Proves what?" asked Pooh, who was still thinking about honey.

"It proves that Wednesday doesn't always follow Tuesday. Sometimes Christmas comes the day after Tuesday."

"Oh," said Pooh. "I hadn't thought about that."

"Could today be Christmas?" Piglet was suddenly very worried because if it was, he was very far behind in his preparations.

"I . . . don't . . . think . . . so," said Pooh slowly. "Because on Christmas, in my experience, there is usually snow on the ground, and there isn't." He looked around very carefully to make sure that there wasn't a little patch of snow somewhere that he had missed. If there was a lit-

tle smidgen of snow just sort of lying around, then maybe it just might be a Christmas of Very Little Snowfall that had somehow crept up on them and he should run home to see if there was a large gift of honey waiting for him.

"No," said Piglet, also looking around, although he was thinking about haycorns. "There isn't."

"So, if it isn't Christmas, it must be Wednesday."

"I suppose so, but I'm not really sure." Piglet looked under the nearest bush to see if there might be snow there, and there wasn't so he looked all around. "Look, Pooh, there's Tigger coming. Why don't we ask him if today is Christmas or Wednesday?"

Tigger was Bouncing along pretending to hunt What-ever-It-Was that Tiggers hunted. Since he wasn't quite sure what "IT" was that Tiggers hunted, he was practicing on anything that he came upon. He would Bounce along until he saw something that looked likely and then he would get down very low to the ground and creep closer very carefully so as not to alert Whatever-It-Was.

When Piglet and Pooh came up to him, he was stalking a very large gorse-bush. "Hallo, Tigger," they said.

"Shhhhh," said Tigger very quietly. "I'm hunting a fierce Something-Or-Other. I'll be with you in just a minute." As Piglet and Pooh watched, Tigger slowly moved forward, keeping close to the ground, his tail twitching rapidly back and forth. Then with a loud *Worraworraworraworraworra* he jumped into the very middle of the gorse-bush, thrashed and rolled around, and, after a terrible struggle, managed to pull himself out, all covered with prickles.

"Have I won?" he asked cheerfully.

"That's just a harmless gorse-bush," said Pooh.

"If it's harmless, why did it bite me when I wasn't looking?"

"I don't think it did."

"Yes it did. It would have bitten me worse but I was too quick for it. See, I have bites all over."

"Those are just prickles," said Pooh. "You always get prickles if you happen to get into a gorse-bush."

"Maybe Tiggers don't hunt gorse-bushes." Tigger looked carefully at the gorse-bush so as to remember that it wasn't the Sort-Of-Thing that Tiggers hunted.

"I suspect not," said Pooh, as he and Piglet began to help Tigger get rid of the prickles. "They aren't even good to eat. The only one I know who might like to eat them would be Eeyore, who likes prickly things like Thistles." After they had gotten most of the prickles out of Tigger and he was feeling Bouncy again, Piglet, from behind Pooh, because he was a Very Small Animal and being Bounced on might seriously damage him, asked, "Tigger, is today Wednesday?"

"Or is it Christmas?" asked Pooh. Hoping that there still might be a small chance that it was.

Tigger considered this, first sitting down and then getting up rather quickly to remove a prickle that they had missed and then sitting down again.

"I think," he said at last, "that it can't be Christmas, because, if it were, we would all be over at Christopher Robin's house helping him open his presents like we do every year. So it must be Wednesday. Why do you want to know?"

"Because The Stranger said he would see me tomorrow and he isn't here." Pooh didn't have to explain about The Stranger because everyone in the Forest knew about him by now.

"Well, that explains it," said Tigger. "It's not tomorrow. It's today. You're a day early, Pooh."

"Not really," said Pooh. "Because he said it yesterday and yesterday's tomorrow is today and not tomorrow, just like tomorrow's yesterday would be today." He paused to make sure that he had gotten it right. "Which is Wednesday, you see, if it isn't Christmas, because yesterday I took jumping lessons from Kanga, which always happens on Tuesdays."

"If The Stranger is supposed to be here, and he isn't," said Tigger, looking around, "then he must be Someplace Else." Pooh and Piglet thought about that and agreed that Tigger was probably right.

"Maybe he's lost," squeaked Piglet.

"If that's so," said Pooh, remembering about Establishing Objectives and Organizing, "our objective should be to find him. Since there are three of us, we will all go in different directions because that way we will have a better chance to find him."

"If he is lost," said Piglet, trying to keep out of the way of Tigger by moving around Pooh, "instead of thinking that tomorrow is tomorrow. That is."

Pooh was too busy Organizing to listen. "Piglet, since you have the shortest legs, you will look at the closest Someplace Else, which would be around Rabbit's and Eeyore's houses. I'll go over and look in the Hundred Acre Wood, which is the next closest Someplace Else. Tigger, you look on the other side of the Forest near the bee-tree."

Then Pooh reviewed their assignments with them to make certain that each knew exactly where to go.

"After we have looked, we'll meet back here just before lunch." That was just in case The Stranger had brought his picnic basket with him.

So they all set off in their proper directions.

Pooh was the first to return because Piglet had found a Very Nice Patch of haycorns and that had delayed his search. When he saw Piglet coming along, munching on the last of the haycorns, he called out, "Did you find The Stranger?" thinking that perhaps carrying a Very Heavy picnic basket might have caused him to lag behind Piglet.

"No," said Piglet. "I did find a Very Nice Patch of haycorns, so it wasn't a complete waste. Did you?"

"I didn't find a single haycorn," said Pooh. "If I had I would have brought them back for you."

"I meant, did you find The Stranger?" Piglet looked all around to make certain The Stranger wasn't hiding behind a tree so that he could jump out and say "Surprise!" at Piglet. Piglet was a Very Small Animal and was not too fond of People jumping out unexpectedly.

"No," said Pooh. "Let's hope that Tigger found him." So they settled down to wait. Pooh kept glancing at the sun, which was almost overhead, although he really didn't have to since his stomach told him it was almost lunchtime.

After what seemed to be a long time, but really wasn't, Tigger came Bouncing along through the trees.

"Did you find The Stranger?" Pooh and Piglet called out together.

"Of course," answered Tigger. "Tiggers always find Strangers if they go looking for them."

"Where is he?" Pooh stretched up as tall as he could to see where The Stranger was, and if he had a heavy picnic basket with him.

"He's over on the other side of the Forest, near the bee-tree, sitting on a rock with his picnic basket beside him."

"Why didn't you bring him back with you?" asked Pooh.

"You didn't say to bring him back," said Tigger reproachfully. "You just said to find him. Which I did. And almost right away. I watched him for a long time, but he didn't do anything except sit there. I was behind a bush, so he didn't see me. Tiggers are very cunning about things like that, you know."

"Well, if you found him right away, why didn't you

come right back and tell us so we wouldn't waste our time looking Someplace Else when he wasn't there?"

Tigger shook his head. "You didn't say to find him and come right back. You said to find him and then we would meet here just before lunch. Which is now. I remember distinctly you said that."

"Bother! You misunderstood me," said Pooh.

"If you didn't mean what you said," Tigger pointed out logically, "then you should say what you mean."

"Well, there's no helping it now. We'll just have to go over to the bee-tree." Pooh shook his head sadly.

"Since it's lunchtime now, he probably will have eaten everything in his picnic basket by the time we get there. Oh, bother!"

Fortunately, he hadn't.

While they were eating lunch, which included some gourmet haycorns for Piglet, imported Extract of Malt for Tigger, and, of course, a large pot of honey for Pooh, The Stranger was told about the difficulties they had had in finding him.

"It seems to me as if there were problems with communication," he said. "In a way, that is fortunate, because that is one of the things we are going to talk about today."

"What's communication?" asked Piglet, who hadn't been with Pooh when it had been talked about.

"It means telling everyone working on a project what is happening. Everyone needs to communicate,

because that's how we learn and
live. From the information we receive, we make decisions about
what to do, what not to do, how to
work, how to live, how others are
relating to us, what they are
thinking and feeling, and what is important to them.

"From the information we give, others learn the
same things.

"Which is why communication is so important to a
manager. It is a manager's job to get things done, and the
only way that things get done is by an exchange of information. If a manager is not good at communicating, individuals will not understand what is wanted. They will not
know how to direct their efforts in trying to achieve the
objectives that have been set, and they will not know how
they are doing. Since others working with them will have
the same problem, there will be duplication of effort or,
even worse, some necessary things will not get done at all."

"Are there rules?" asked Pooh. "I like rules. Then I
know if I am doing things in the correct manner."

"Yes," answered The Stranger. "Suppose I tell you
the rules and then you can tell me why you had difficulties this morning."

"Do the rules apply to Tiggers?" asked Tigger.

"They apply to everyone who needs to exchange information, which, by the way, is another definition of
communication."

"Good!" Tigger sat up straighter. "Tiggers like to communicate."

"That's fortunate," said The Stranger. "If you like something, you will tend to be good at it."

"Tiggers are Very Good at communication," said Tigger in a very decided voice.

"The nice thing about communication is that almost anyone can improve her performance and become a better communicator."

"If she follows the rules," said Piglet.

"Yes. Which brings us to the first rule." The Stranger took a large tablet from his picnic basket and wrote down the first rule in big letters. When he had finished, he showed it to the others and read it aloud.

1. TO COMMUNICATE THERE MUST BE AN EXCHANGE OF INFORMATION.

"This rule says several things. There must be at least two individuals. There can be many individuals involved in the communication, but there must be at least two. Next there must be an exchange of information. That means that all communication should be a two-way process—back and forth, if you like, with all individuals who are participating both getting and giving information."

"Does that mean," asked Pooh, "that if I am telling

Tigger that he should search the other side of the Forest, I should be getting information from him also?"

"Absolutely. At the very least he should give you the information that he knows what he is to do and that he will do it."

"That's so I will know that I communicated properly."

"Exactly. The word for it is 'Feedback,' which we'll talk about after we've covered the other rules.

"Now the second rule is this:

2. ALL INFORMATION EXCHANGED SHOULD BE AS CLEAR AND COMPLETE AS POSSIBLE.

"There is a law called 'Murphy's Law' that states: 'If anything can be misunderstood, it will be misunderstood.' There are many reasons why we don't understand information that we receive. One reason is that the same word or words mean different things to different people."

"Like when Owl said, 'On the other hand—' and I thought he meant what he said, but what he really meant was 'As distinguished from,' " said Pooh.

"That's a good example," said The Stranger. "Let me give you another in the form of a little game."

"Good," squeaked Piglet. "I like games."

"I will say a word, and then you each tell me what that word meant to you. Ready? The word is 'house.' "

Tigger said, "Kanga's."

Piglet said, "Eeyore's."

Pooh said, "Owl's."

"We have three different meanings then for the one word 'house.' Why did you pick those words for your answer?"

"I live at Kanga's house," answered Tigger. "So I thought of her house."

"I was remembering when Pooh and I built a house for Eeyore," said Piglet. "It's the only house I ever built, so I thought of that."

"And I thought of Owl's because it is a Very Grand Indeed house, and I was just talking about Owl saying 'On the other hand,' which happened at his house." Pooh paused for a moment and then said, "Communication is very difficult if the same word means different things to different people."

"Did I win?" asked Tigger.

"Yes. You all had very reasonable answers," said The Stranger.

"Good," said Tigger. "I like to win games."

"You can see from this that if I asked you all to meet me at the house, it is very likely that we would all end up in a different place—just because the same word has different meanings to different people. So you must be careful with the words that you use."

"It seems to me that there must be other reasons," said Piglet. "Even when I use words that we all know, I sometimes have problems."

"Yes. Another very common reason that causes problems is that people don't always pay attention. This is particularly true with verbal communication. The problem is that we can think much faster than someone can talk, so our minds tend to wander, and we miss parts of the information even though we think we are listening carefully."

"I'm sorry," interrupted Pooh. "I didn't hear that last part. I was watching the bees in the bee-tree and thinking they must be making lots of honey because they are buzzing very loudly." So The Stranger repeated what he had said, and Pooh was a Very Embarrassed Bear. However, The Stranger said it was all right because it Proved the Point.

"Of course," The Stranger continued, "all of your information should be complete. The danger here is that, as a manager, you are so familiar with what you want to communicate, you might leave something out. So you need to review carefully everything you will be communicating to make certain it is complete."

"Like Pooh not saying that I was to bring you back," said Tigger. "When I found you, that is."

"Yes. That's a good example. Now we come to a very important rule that is often overlooked." The Stranger wrote it on his tablet.

3. THE INFORMATION SHOULD BE MEAN-INGFUL TO THE INDIVIDUAL WHO IS RECEIVING IT.

"There are really two reasons for this rule. The first is that even if the information is clear and complete, the individual who is receiving the information will not pay much attention to it unless it is meaningful, or you could say 'important,' to him. As the saying goes, 'It goes in one ear and out the other.'

"Now, you probably wouldn't be bothering to communicate the information unless you felt that it was important to those who were receiving it, so you must express it in a way that stresses what is important to them.

"For instance, if you are managing a factory and there is the need to increase production because you are not meeting delivery dates that your customers require, you could call your people together and tell them that. However, that probably isn't very meaningful to most of them, so they won't pay attention, or they won't take it very seriously, figuring that is the sales department's problem.

"On the other hand—"

"He means as distinguished from the first thing," Pooh whispered to Piglet.

"If you tell them that the customers may cancel their orders unless delivery is improved, and if that happens, there may have to be layoffs, you can be sure you will have their attention, because now the information is important to them.

"The second reason is that there is not much point in telling someone something that is not of importance to her. You are just wasting her time and yours."

"Sometimes Eeyore goes on at great length about the new Thistle patch he has found," said Pooh. "I am glad he found it, of course, but really, I am not all that interested in Thistles."

"What do you do when that happens?"

"I usually think about what I would do if I found a big pot of honey." Pooh shook his head. "Honey is much more difficult to find than Thistles. Then when I realize that Eeyore has stopped talking about Thistles, I pay attention again."

"You see, that is exactly what the rule guards against."

"Are there more rules?" asked Tigger. He was beginning to Bounce.

"There are two more, and they are Very Important." The Stranger wrote down the next rule in even bigger letters than he had before.

4. ALWAYS GET CONFIRMATION THAT THE MESSAGE YOU ARE COMMUNICAT- ING HAS BEEN UNDERSTOOD.

"This is called 'feedback.' It means that because of all the reasons we have been talking about, you should always make certain that the message you were communicating was understood. You do this by asking those to whom you are giving the information to tell you what information they received and by listening Very, Very Carefully to what they tell you.

"If what they tell you is not correct, then you tell them what they have not understood or have missed, and you repeat this process until you are certain they have understood your message. You see, to be a good communicator, you must be a good listener."

"Tiggers are Very Good Listeners," said Tigger. "That's why I know that Pooh didn't say to bring you back when I found you."

"And I didn't ask for feedback from him," said Pooh. "That's where I went wrong. I fear I am a Bear of Very Little Brain."

"But then you didn't know the rule," pointed out The Stranger.

"That's true," said Pooh. "I would do much better now."

"So now we come to the last rule."

5. INFORMATION CAN BE GIVEN IN MANY WAYS. THE MORE WAYS YOU USE, THE CLEARER AND MORE BELIEVABLE IT

WILL BE. HOWEVER, THE MESSAGE MUST BE THE SAME IN ALL WAYS. IT IS VITAL TO BE CONSISTENT.

Pooh, Piglet, and Tigger looked at the rule carefully.

"I . . . don't . . . understand . . . it," Piglet said finally. "I thought if you had a message for someone, you just told them." Then he quickly added, "Making sure that it is clear, complete, and meaningful, of course."

"And getting feedback," Pooh added. "That's very important."

"Well," said The Stranger, "there are really many ways that we use to communicate and to get our messages across.

"We are using two right now. We are talking about the rules of communication. That's called giving information verbally—in other words, we hear the information. At the same time, I am writing it down on this tablet, so we can see it. That's called giving information visually—we see it.

"Then we could combine those two ways so that we give the information in two forms at the same time—as in a movie or a TV program. That's really a third way.

"The most important way, particularly for a manager, is information given by the way he acts. The individuals who are receiving the information will watch him closely to see if the way he acts gives the same message that he is giving by other ways such as verbally or visually. If his actions convey a message that is different from what he is saying or writing, they will assume that he really doesn't mean what he is saying or writing."

"I still don't understand," said Piglet, "about the acting part, that is, and giving information by what you do."

"Let's take an example, then. Suppose you are a manager, and you notice that the place where everyone works is not clean or neat. You know it is important, because when things are messy, it is not very nice to be there and you often can't find things when they are needed."

"I was clean once," interrupted Piglet. "Kanga gave me a bath when I was pretending to be Roo." He thought for a moment. "I didn't like it very much. Being clean, that is. It wasn't comfortable and it changed my color."

"We were talking about the place where everyone works," said Pooh. "Not about the ones who work there."

"Oh," said Piglet. "Excuse me. Please go on."

"So the manager calls everyone together and shows them how messy everything is, points out how much nicer it will be if it is clean and neat and how their work will be easier if the situation is changed. He then asks for their suggestions about what should be done and incorporates their ideas into his own plan. He organizes the work, writes it down, gives everyone a copy, posts it on the bulletin board, and gets feedback to make sure that it is understood."

"So then the place became clean and neat," said Tigger. "I like happy endings."

"Unfortunately, it didn't."

"I don't see why it didn't," said Pooh. "It seems to me that the manager followed all the rules."

"It didn't because the manager made a mistake that undid all the good work he had done. He didn't clean up his own office, which had dust balls in all the corners, papers falling off his desk, and books and folders piled on top of file cabinets. He also crumpled up a piece of paper when he was out in the shop where everyone was working and just threw it on the floor. So everyone decided from his actions that being clean and neat was not really very important and didn't do anything themselves."

"I see," said Piglet. "You could say that actions speak louder than words."

"That's very good, Piglet. I'll just add it to the last rule."

"It's original too," said Piglet proudly. "I just thought it up."

The Stranger wrote down what Piglet had said and added a title at the beginning so that what was written on the tablet looked like this:

RULES FOR EFFECTIVE COMMUNICATION

1. TO COMMUNICATE THERE MUST BE AN EXCHANGE OF INFORMATION.
2. ALL INFORMATION EXCHANGED SHOULD BE AS CLEAR AND COMPLETE AS POSSIBLE.
3. THE INFORMATION SHOULD BE MEANINGFUL TO THE INDIVIDUAL WHO IS RECEIVING IT.
4. ALWAYS GET CONFIRMATION THAT THE MESSAGE YOU ARE COMMUNICATING HAS BEEN UNDERSTOOD.
5. INFORMATION CAN BE GIVEN IN MANY WAYS. THE MORE WAYS YOU USE, THE CLEARER AND MORE BELIEVABLE IT WILL BE. HOWEVER, THE MESSAGE MUST BE THE SAME IN ALL WAYS. IT IS VITAL TO BE CONSISTENT. REMEMBER, ACTIONS SPEAK LOUDER THAN WORDS.

They all looked at the list written on the tablet.

"I can see why we had difficulty this morning," Pooh said at last. "We didn't follow the rule about information being as clear and complete as possible, and we didn't get feedback."

· "Exactly," said The Stranger. "It was a good example of why the manager must be very careful when she is communicating and must think about it before she does it and while she is doing it. All managers should practice the rules until they become second nature."

"I'm not going to practice hunting now," said Tigger. "I'm going to find Eeyore and practice communication." With a loud *Worraworraworraworraworra* he Bounced off in the direction of Eeyore's house.

"Thank you," said Piglet to The Stranger. "I'm sure that things will be much clearer from now on. I think I'll go see Owl and find out if he can communicate to me where he might have seen a patch of haycorns recently." He started off toward the Hundred Acre Wood.

After Tigger and Piglet had left, The Stranger and Pooh agreed that they would meet the next day. They made very certain this time that they followed the rules of communication, and The Stranger complimented Pooh on his Particularly Excellent use of feedback.

It was only after The Stranger had left that Pooh realized that he hadn't sung his Manager Song. "I am a Very Forgetful Bear," he said to himself. "I forgot it again. Oh, bother!"

V

In which Pooh Finally Sings His Manager Song, Eeyore Wanders By, an Expotition Is Remembered, and Motivation, Delegation, and Leadership Are Explored

Pooh was a Very Determined Bear. Twice he had forgotten to sing his Manager Song to The Stranger. This morning he would not forget because it was an Important Song. It was Important because it was to remind himself to ask The Stranger about words like "leader" and "delegate," and how they fit into a manager's job.

The best way not to forget was to sing the song to himself all the way from his house until he saw The Stranger. So, as he walked along through the heather, he sang the song to himself.

> *The manager, manager,*
> *A leader must be.*
> *That's Most Important,*
> *As we all can see.*

After he had sung it over and over, he
tried humming it, but somehow it didn't
make a very good Hum, so he went back
to singing it. He went on singing it until
he came to the part of the stream where
the stepping-stones were, and when he
was in the middle of the third stone,
he began to wonder why the song did not
feel like a Good Song. So he sat down on the stone in the
middle of the stream and thought about it.

The sun was so delightfully warm, and the stone,
which had been sitting in it for a long time, was so
warm too that Pooh almost forgot to think about the
song, but then he remembered that he had to meet The
Stranger and that the song should be a Good Song lest
The Stranger would think that he didn't deserve to become a V.I.B.

"It seems to me," he said, "that since the song is
about a Very Important Thing and is used to remind me
about Very Important Words, it should be a Very Important Song."

He watched a dragonfly hover overhead while he
thought about that. "Bother! The trouble is, it doesn't
sound like a Very Important Song."

He sang it again, Just To Be Sure. The dragonfly
darted away, which proved that it wasn't a Very Important Song, because if it had been, the dragonfly would
surely have stayed to see how it came out.

"It seems to me," thought Pooh, "that if it is to be a Very Important Song, it should be longer." So he made up some more for the song.

> *He delegates work*
> *To those that he trusts.*
> *Objectives and organizing*
> *Are some of his musts.*

Pooh decided that the second verse made the song a more Important one, so he got up off his stone and went to meet The Stranger.

As he walked, he thought that if one more verse

made the song seem more Important, then a third verse might make it seem Very Important, which was what was wanted. So, as he walked, he wiped his mouth with the back of his paw to remove a little something left over from the little something of marmalade and honey he had had for breakfast and sang a rather fluffy third verse through the fur. It went like this:

> *He does all these things*
> *As well as he can.*
> *For they are all part*
> *Of a manager's plan.*

Written down like this, it doesn't seem like a Very Important Song, but coming through pale fawn fluff at about half-past nine on a very sunny morning, it seemed to Pooh to be one of the Most Important Songs he had ever sung. So he went on singing it all the way to where The Stranger was waiting for him.

"Hallo, Pooh," said The Stranger. "Did you make up that song?"

"Well, I sort of made it up," said Pooh. "It isn't Brain," he went on humbly, "because it just sort of comes to me, you know, so I can remember to ask you about what Owl said is important. Which is a manager being a leader and delegating."

"Those are important and it seems to me that your song is Very Appropriate. We were going to talk about motivation today. We can cover leadership and delegation at the same time."

"Oh," said Pooh. "Thank you. About the song, I mean." Pooh was not quite sure what "Appropriate" meant, but it sounded Important. He then told The Stranger all about his conversation with Owl or at least the part he had forgotten to tell him about last time.

"I am pretty certain about delegation," he finished, "but I'm not sure what a leader is, and why it is important that a manager should be a leader."

"Well," said The Stranger, "why don't we see if you can think of an adventure that had a leader, and we can see what that tells us about what a leader is."

"It's hard to think of an adventure that had a leader if one is not sure what a leader is," pointed out Pooh in a Very Reasonable tone of voice.

"That's a very good point. A leader is an individual who goes ahead and others follow."

"Oh," said Pooh. "That kind of an adventure. I remember—" but he had to stop because, just at that moment, Eeyore wandered into sight, saw Pooh and The Stranger talking, and came over to them.

"Hallo, Pooh," he said. "I found my tail just where you said. It was pretending to be a bell-pull, but it couldn't fool me." Eeyore looked back at his tail, which was following close behind him.

"That's a very fine tail," said The Stranger, and introduced himself.

"As tails go, I suppose it's all right," said Eeyore sadly. "Actually, tails are supposed to go where the individual who is attached to them goes, and this one doesn't. Not always. Sometimes it goes and becomes a bell-pull. It's just my luck to have a tail that wants to be a bell-pull." After a long silence he added, "How like a tail." He looked back to make sure it was still there.

"That reminds me," said Pooh. "We were just talking about a tale. The one where we all went on an Expotition to discover the North Pole and Christopher Robin was our leader."

"I remember that," Eeyore said gloomily. "It didn't end very well. Speaking of end, you will remember what happened to my tail in that adventure, won't you?"

"Of course," said Pooh. "But that happened later. I'll tell it from the beginning so The Stranger will understand it."

"Very well," said Eeyore. "Just so you don't forget. Some do, you know. Forget their promises, that is."

Pooh promised not to forget the part about Eeyore's tail and began at the beginning.

"It all began with me meeting Christopher Robin," said Pooh.

Christopher Robin was sitting outside his door, putting on his Big Boots. As soon as he saw the Big Boots, Pooh knew that an Adventure was going to happen, and he brushed the honey off his nose with the back of his paw, and spruced himself up as well as he could, so as to look Ready for Anything.

"Good-morning, Christopher Robin," he called out.

"Hallo, Pooh Bear. I can't get this boot on."

"That's bad," said Pooh. "Do you think you could very kindly lean against me, 'cos I keep pulling so hard that I fall over backwards."

Pooh sat down, dug his feet into the ground, and pushed hard against Christopher Robin's back, and Christopher Robin pushed hard against his, and pulled and pulled at his boot until he had got it on.

"A good leader involves others in his preparations," said The Stranger. "What did he tell you then?"

"Then he told me this," said Pooh.

"We are all going on an Expedition," said Christopher Robin, as he got up and brushed himself. "Thank you, Pooh."

"Going on an Expotition?" said Pooh eagerly. "I don't

think I've ever been on one of those. Where are we going to on this Expotition?"

"Expedition, silly old Bear. It's got an 'x' in it."

"Oh!" said Pooh. "I know." But he didn't really.

"We're going to discover the North Pole."

"Oh!" said Pooh again. "What *is* the North Pole?" he asked.

"It's just a thing you discover," said Christopher Robin carelessly, not being quite sure himself.

"Oh! I see," said Pooh. "Are bears any good at discovering it?"

"Of course they are. And Rabbit and Kanga and all of you. It's an Expedition. That's what an Expedition means. A long line of everybody. . . .

"That sounded as if it would be exciting," Pooh said.

"A good leader will always try to make the project that she wants worked on seem to be exciting," said The Stranger. "That is really part of motivating individuals. Everyone will try to do a better job when they feel that the project is exciting and significant. By being part of something that is important, individuals will feel that they are important—and everyone likes to feel that way."

"I wasn't sure what a North Pole was," said Pooh, "but Christopher Robin said it was a thing you discover and that sounded important. He also said that bears were good at discovering it."

"That's another thing that leaders do. They encourage and praise those who are working with them. We all like to live up to what someone thinks about us if it is good, so we will try harder to make the project or the work successful. Motivating really means giving someone a reason to do good work. Feeling that a task is important and living up to the good opinion that someone we respect has of us are both very strong reasons to do a good job.

"What did Christopher Robin do then?" The Stranger asked.

"He said this."

> "You'd better tell the others to get ready, while I see if my gun's all right. And we must all bring Provisions."
> "Bring what?"
> "Things to eat."
> "Oh!" said Pooh happily. "I thought you said Provisions. I'll go and tell them." And he stumped off.

"So that was some more motivation for you to join in the Expedition."

"Yes," said Pooh dreamily. "I had a large pot of honey and—"

"What happened next?" asked Eeyore. "I wasn't there, you know. Not at the Beginning. I almost never am. I know what they say. Eeyore doesn't have to be in at the start. He'll come along anyway. Let Eeyore bring up the end." Eeyore sighed. "That's just the way things are. Sad but true."

"When Christopher Robin asked you to tell the

others to get ready," asked The Stranger, "what do you think he was doing?"

Pooh thought for a moment. "I . . . guess . . . he . . . was . . . delegating," he said slowly.

"Exactly. He was giving you a part of his responsibilities to carry out, so that he would have time to do other things. What did you do then?"

"Well, the first person I met was Rabbit, and I told him about the Expotition and what the purpose was and that we were to bring things to eat and that we were to meet at Christopher Robin's. Then I asked him to go tell Kanga, while I went to find Piglet."

"So you delegated part of your task to Rabbit."

"Yes," said Pooh proudly. "I guess I did. Delegate, that is. I can see why Owl said delegation is important. It made my job easier and it got done faster."

"That's why managers use delegation as a very important tool. It allows them to multiply their efforts. You also did it the right way. You told Rabbit the objective and the reasons for the assignment. You gave him an important task to do—many managers delegate only unimportant or minor tasks, which is unfair to those they manage.

"What is even better is that you didn't tell him how to do it. You let him decide how to accomplish the task. If a manager delegates in that way, it gives subordinates a chance to learn and develop their own skills and abilities—to grow by doing parts of the boss's job."

"He didn't do it exactly right," said Pooh. "He brought all of his friends-and-relations, and I only told him to bring Kanga."

"That's not bad. A manager has to learn that when she delegates, those she delegates to may make mistakes. In fact, they almost always will. That is an important part of anyone's development and growth. By making mistakes you learn how to do things right, and you are not afraid to try new things.

"Remember, good judgment is the result of experience, and experience is the result of bad judgment."

"Anyway," said Pooh, "it didn't matter. Rabbit said they could march at the end, after Eeyore."

"It mattered to me," said Eeyore. "I found it unsettling. "But nobody cared because just then Christopher Robin said to come on, and we all went off after him in the order we were in. I was at the end, but I wasn't at the end."

"But you said it was all right," said Pooh.

"Yes, but I also said Don't Blame Me."

"What happened then?" asked The Stranger.

"I made up a song as we walked along," said Pooh, "and I was singing my song to Piglet when suddenly—"

"Hush!" said Christopher Robin turning round to Pooh, "we're just coming to a Dangerous Place. . . ."

"Hush!" said Piglet to Kanga.

"Hush!" said Kanga to Owl, while Roo said "Hush!" several times to himself very quietly.

"Hush!" said Owl to Eeyore.

"*Hush!*" said Eeyore in a terrible voice to all Rabbit's friends-and-relations, and "Hush!" they said hastily to each other all down the line, until it got to the last one of all. And the last and smallest friend-and-relation was so upset to find that the whole Expotition was saying "Hush!" to *him*, that he buried himself head downwards in a crack in the ground, and stayed there for two days until the danger was over, and then went home in a great hurry, and lived quietly with his Aunt ever-afterwards. His name was Alexander Beetle.

They had come to a stream which twisted and tumbled between high rocky banks, and Christopher Robin saw at once how dangerous it was.

"It's just the place," he explained, "for an Ambush."

"Well, I wasn't sure what kind of a bush Christopher Robin had said, so I whispered to Piglet, 'What sort of bush? A gorse-bush?' "

"Owl heard and said that an Ambush was a sort of Surprise. I told him that so is a gorse-bush sometimes. Then Owl said that if people jump out at you suddenly, that's an Ambush, and I told him about the time that a gorse-bush had sprung at me suddenly one day when I fell out of a tree and that it had taken me six days to get all the prickles out of myself. Owl said that we were not talking about gorse-bushes, but I told him that I was."

"We got past the Dangerous Place without an Ambush," said Eeyore. "Now we are almost at the interesting place in the Expo—what we did."

They were climbing very cautiously up the stream now, going from rock to rock, and after they had gone a little way they came to a place where the banks widened out at each side, so that on each side of the water there was a level strip of grass on which they could sit down and rest. As soon as he saw this, Christopher Robin called "Halt!" and they all sat down and rested.

"I think," said Christopher Robin, "that we ought to eat all our Provisions now, so that we shan't have so much to carry."

"That shows that Christopher Robin was a good leader," The Stranger said. "A leader has a sincere interest and concern for the people he manages. One way he shows this is by making certain that their needs are taken care of and that he is concerned for their well-being."

"My need was not taken care of," said Eeyore. "As Usual. Nobody told me to bring along something. How like Them. Nobody even offered to share."

"I shared," said Pooh. "I had by ac-  cident sat down on a thistle, and I got up rather quickly so you could eat it. So you could eat it and for another reason." Pooh rubbed his sitting down place as he remembered the thistle.

"Thank you again, Pooh," said Eeyore. "That was very kind of you to share. As I told you at the time, however, sitting on them doesn't do them any good. Takes all the life out of them. Everyone should remember that and take care not to sit on a thistle if they encounter one. They could call me and I would advise them as to proper behavior toward a thistle."

"I'll remember that," said The Stranger. "What happened next?"

"Well," said Pooh, "Christopher Robin was off talking to Rabbit about the North Pole being a pole because it wouldn't be called a pole if it wasn't. Piglet was lying on his back sleeping peacefully. Roo was washing his face and paws in the stream, while Kanga explained to everybody proudly that this was the first time he had ever washed his face himself. . . ."

"I was saying that I didn't hold with all this washing," said Eeyore. "This modern Behind-the-Ears nonsense. You can't tell what may happen. Bound to be unhealthy, I say. Look what did happen."

"What did happen?" The Stranger asked.

"Roo fell into the stream," said Pooh, "and was being swept downstream over a waterfall into the next pool."

"So much for washing," said Eeyore.

"Everybody was doing something to help," Pooh went on. "Piglet was jumping up and down and making 'Ooo, I say' noises; Owl was explaining that in a case of Sudden and Temporary Immersion, the Important Thing was to keep the Head above Water; Kanga was jumping along the bank, saying 'Are you sure you're all right, Roo dear?' Roo was answering, 'Look at me swimming!' "

"This is the important part," said Eeyore. "I didn't lose my head. I turned around so that I wouldn't be distracted and hung my tail into the pool where Roo had fallen. I told him to catch onto it and he'd be all right."

"That was very quick thinking," said The Stranger.

"Yes," said Eeyore modestly. "I thought so at the time."

"But by that time, Roo had been swept two pools farther down the stream," said Pooh.

"I couldn't have known that," said Eeyore. "After all, I had my back to everything. It is very difficult, in case you've never noticed, to hang your tail in a pool while you are facing it."

"I suppose that's true," said Pooh. "Anyway, I went down two pools below where Roo was and found a long pole, and Kanga came up and took one end of it. We held it across the lower part of the pool, and Roo drifted up against it and climbed out."

"So Roo was rescued," said The Stranger.

"Yes, and something else happened. Christopher Robin came up and asked me where I had found the pole. I told him that I just found it. I thought it ought to be useful so I just picked it up."

"Pooh," said Christopher Robin solemnly, "the Expedition is over. You have found the North Pole!"

"That is all very nice," said Eeyore, "but I was sitting with my tail in the water."

Eeyore took his tail out of the water, and swished it from side to side.

"As I expected," he said. "Lost all feeling. Numbed it. That's what it's done. Numbed it. Well, as long as nobody minds, I suppose it's all right."

"Poor old Eeyore. I'll dry it for you," said Christopher Robin, and he took out his handkerchief and rubbed it up.

"Thank you, Christopher Robin. You're the only one who seems to understand about tails. They don't think— that's what's the matter with some of these others. They've no imagination. A tail isn't a tail to *them*, it's just a Little Bit Extra at the back."

"Never mind, Eeyore," said Christopher Robin, rubbing his hardest. "Is *that* better?"

"It's feeling more like a tail perhaps. It Belongs again, if you know what I mean."

"That's another characteristic of a leader," said The Stranger. "He treats individuals as individuals. He doesn't treat those with tails the same as he does those without tails. What else happened?"

They stuck the pole in the ground, and Christopher Robin tied a message on to it.

NORTH POLE
DISCOVERED BY POOH
POOH FOUND IT.

"That was very nice of Christopher Robin to do that," said The Stranger after admiring the message. "You see, Pooh, that is another thing that a good leader does. He gives credit to others. Since he was the leader of the Expedition, he could have said that he discovered the North Pole. Our natural tendency is to make ourselves look good. An effective leader's goal is to make his *people* look good."

"It made me feel proud of what I had done," said Pooh. "It made me feel so good I went home and had a little something to revive myself." Pooh looked at the picnic basket again, and this time The Stranger noticed.

As he unpacked the picnic basket, The Stranger continued talking. "I would say that Christopher Robin was a very good leader. First, he created an air of excitement about the job that was to be done. Then he kept the objective as simple as possible so that everyone could understand what needed to be done."

"Even Piglet," said Pooh, watching the basket being unpacked.

"Even Piglet," The Stranger agreed. "He acted as a role model—showing by his actions how he expected others to act. He treated individuals as individuals—with dignity and respect—and showed he was concerned with their welfare. When something happened like Roo falling in the stream, he stood out of the way and let the others get on with their job, not interfering unless he was really needed, because a leader's job is to lead, not to do. Finally, he gave credit to you, when he could have taken it himself."

"Yes," said Pooh. "I didn't know it was the North

Pole when I picked it up. Christopher Robin recognized it so he could have properly said that he discovered it and taken the credit."

"But he didn't, which shows he was a good leader."

Pooh didn't answer because he was too involved with a particularly good jar of honey, which tasted like the bees had made it from apple blossoms, but he nodded to show that he thought Christopher Robin was a Very Good Leader indeed.

VI

In which We Talk About Measuring Ents, a Woozle Is Tracked to Its Lair and Defined, and Pooh Gets to Know How Much Honey He Has

Pooh was sitting in his house counting his pots of honey.

Waking up early that morning, just as the sun came in through the window and made interesting patterns on the floor, the Thought Had Occurred that it had been several days since The Stranger with his picnic basket had been in the Forest.

Once the Thought Had Occurred, another thought came right along behind it. If The Stranger hadn't come to the Forest in several days, he might not come with his picnic basket for several more days.

Pooh sat up in bed and watched the dust motes dance in the sunbeams. It seemed to him that the two thoughts were Significant. "Perhaps," he said to himself, "if I had a little something, All Would become Clear." So he got out of bed, selected a pot of honey from his honey-cupboard, and sat down at the table to think about the Thoughts.

As everyone knows, it is very difficult to think about Significant Thoughts when one is eating honey. So it was not until he had finished the pot of honey and was looking inside to see if just possibly a Little More might have been hidden away in a corner that he realized why the Thoughts were Significant.

If The Stranger hadn't come to the Forest for several days, he might not come for several days more, and if he didn't come he wouldn't be bringing his picnic basket, and that was Significant. Without the picnic basket there wouldn't be any more extra pots of honey, and he, Pooh, would have to depend upon his own supply. The Thing to Do was to count how many pots he had in his honey-cupboard.

Pooh did this from time to time, anyway, even when there was no really good reason to do so, just because it was sort of comforting to be able to say to himself "I've got fifteen pots of honey left. Or sixteen, as the case may be."

He had found from experience that it was not nearly so comforting to say "I've got one pot of honey left," and to say "I've got no pots of honey left" was distinctly Uncomforting and Upsetting, so he usually waited to count until his larder was full.

This particular day, his larder was Very Full because The Stranger had brought so many pots of honey on his visits and had so nicely offered to share, even suggesting that Pooh take leftovers home, that Pooh had not used much of his own honey.

When the honey-cupboard was not full, Pooh could count the pots while they were in the cupboard because he kept them all on the bottom shelf where they were Easy to Reach.

When it was full, counting was a much more difficult task. He could never remember whether one counted the pots on one shelf and multiplied by three, or counted what was on each shelf and then added them all together. Since Pooh was really only sure of Times Twos, he usually decided to add, and even that was difficult since he was never sure if eleven added to six was eleventy-six or fourteen.

The best way, when the honey-cupboard was full, was to take all the pots out and put them in a line on the floor.

So he got a chair to stand on and began to move the pots from the cupboard to the floor.

When he had them all nicely arranged in an almost straight line, he began to count. He did very well until he came to the next to the last pot in the line. It was not a full pot. Pooh could look in and see that there was honey in it about halfway up.

"Bother," he said. "If it is a half-full pot, I should count it as half full. If it is half empty, I should count it that way." He finally decided that if he ate the honey, there would be no question. The pot would definitely be empty. So he did and it was.

He was just finishing counting when there came a knock on his door.

"Fourteen," said Pooh. "Come in. Fourteen. Or was it fifteen? Bother! That's muddled me."

"Hallo, Pooh," said The Stranger.

"Hallo. Fourteen, wasn't it?"

"What was?"

"My pots of honey that I was counting."

"Well," said The Stranger, "I heard you saying fifteen when I opened the door—just before you said 'Bother.' "

"Oh," said Pooh. "I guess I did. Now I shall have to count them again."

"Before you do that, why don't you add the three pots of honey I brought along? They are imported: one from France, one from Spain, and one from Italy. I would appreciate the opinion of an expert like you on which is best."

"Thank you very kindly," said Pooh. "The honey I like best comes from bees, but I shall be pleased to help out." And he added the three pots to those that were already on the floor. Since the pots already stretched from wall to wall, he had to start another line. He looked at them and scratched his head.

"Counting is difficult," he said to The Stranger, "unless you have them in a straight line. Even when they are all in a line, it is sometimes hard because all the pots are not the same size, and the question is if you should count two small pots as one big pot."

"I can see how that would be," said The Stranger.

"The thing is, it is more comforting to say that you have sixteen pots of honey, if you count two small ones separately, than if you say you have fifteen pots. But when it comes time to eat them, a small pot is Hardly Enough, so you end up eating two small ones, so it is just like you only had fifteen instead of sixteen."

"So you might as well count the two small ones as one."

"I suppose so." Pooh sighed. "It is comforting though to have an Extra Pot. Just for emergencies, you know, like a snowstorm or a flood when you can't get out to get more."

"An extra pot is comforting," The Stranger agreed.

"Then I had a problem of what to do about a pot that wasn't full and it wasn't empty, but I solved that."

"That's good."

"Yes, it was," said Pooh dreamily, licking his lips.

"It's not really surprising that you find counting difficult," said The Stranger. "Counting is measurement, which, as you remember, is part of a manager's job, and is usually the part that is done the least well by many managers."

"I can understand why," said Pooh, "but I thought it was measuring Ents."

"No, it was measurement. Remember, you stepped on the 'm' and scuffed it out so it looked like it was 'Measure ent.' "

"I am a bear of Very Little Brain. I forgot! But why does a manager bother with measurement? I know you told me, but I forgot that too."

"After a manager has set the objectives for what needs to be accomplished, organized the effort, and motivated the individuals who will be working, she needs to have a way to know what is happening and what progress is being made toward the established objectives. She gets this information by setting up yardsticks or measurements."

"Oh, yes," said Pooh. "Now I remember. Unless people know how they are doing, and what they are doing right, they can't improve their performance, or know if they are making progress toward achieving their objectives. As Eeyore would say, 'They won't know if they are reaching their goal or playing "Here we go gathering Nuts in May" with the end part of an ant's nest.' "

The Stranger smiled. "That's a very good way of describing the way things are if you don't have good measurements. So, a manager will see that everyone concerned has measurements available that not only show how the organization is performing but that also relate directly to the work of each individual.

"You see, Pooh, the manager interprets and analyzes the measurements, shows how they evaluate performance, and communicates this information to everyone—her subordinates, peers, and superiors. Basically, the manager sees that information is available that allows everyone to track the progress that is being made."

Pooh thought for a moment. "Piglet and I tracked something once."

"Why don't you tell me about it, and perhaps it will make this business of measurement clearer."

"Very well," said Pooh, settling down in his most comfortable chair, "although I'm not sure it will. Help, that is. The way it went was like this."

One fine winter's day when Piglet was brushing away the snow in front of his house, he happened to look up, and there was Winnie-the-Pooh. Pooh was walking round and round in a circle, thinking of something else, and when Piglet called to him, he just went on walking.

"Hallo! said Piglet, "what are *you* doing?"

"Hunting," said Pooh.

"Hunting what?"

"Tracking something," said Winnie-the-Pooh very mysteriously.

"Tracking what?" said Piglet, coming closer.

"That's just what I ask myself. I ask myself, What?"

"What do you think you'll answer?"

"I shall have to wait until I catch up with it," said Winnie-the-Pooh. "Now, look there." He pointed to the ground in front of him. "What do you see there?"

"Tracks," said Piglet. "Paw-marks." He gave a little squeak of excitement. "Oh, Pooh! Do you think it's a—a—a Woozle?"

"It may be," said Pooh. "Sometimes it is, and sometimes it isn't. You never can tell with paw-marks."

With these few words he went on tracking, and Piglet, after watching him for a minute or two, ran after him. Winnie-the-Pooh had come to a sudden stop, and was bending over the tracks in a puzzled sort of way.

"What's the matter?" asked Piglet.

"It's a very funny thing," said Bear, "but there seem to be *two* animals now. This—whatever-it-was—has been joined by another—whatever-it-is—and the two of them are now proceeding in company. . . ."

There was a small spinney of larch trees just here, and it seemed as if the two Woozles, if that is what they were, had been going round this spinney; so round this spinney went Pooh and Piglet after them. . . .

Suddenly Winnie-the-Pooh stopped and pointed excitedly in front of him. "*Look!*"

"*What?*" said Piglet, with a jump. And then, to show that he hadn't been frightened, he jumped up and down once or twice in an exercising sort of way.

"The tracks!" said Pooh. "A *third animal has joined the other two!*"

"Pooh!" cried Piglet. "Do you think it is another Woozle?"

"No," said Pooh, "because it makes different marks. It is either Two Woozles and one, as it might be, Wizzle, or Two, as it might be, Wizzles and one, if so it is, Woozle. Let us continue to follow them."

So they went on, feeling just a little anxious now, in case the three animals in front of them were of Hostile Intent. . . . And then, all of a sudden, Winnie-the-Pooh stopped again, and licked the tip of his nose in a cooling manner, for he was feeling more hot and anxious than ever in his life before. *There were four animals in front of them!* . . .

"I *think*," said Piglet, when he had licked the tip of his nose too, and found that it brought very little comfort, "I *think* that I have just remembered something. I have just remembered something that I forgot to do yesterday and shan't be able to do tomorrow. So I suppose I really ought to go back and do it now."

"So you were left to track the Woozles by yourself," said The Stranger.

"Not really," said Pooh.

Pooh looked up at the sky, and then, as he heard the whistle again, he looked up into the branches of a big oak-tree, and then he saw a friend of his.

"It's Christopher Robin," he said. . . .

Christopher Robin came slowly down his tree.

"Silly old Bear," he said, "what *were* you doing? First you went round the spinney twice by yourself, and then Piglet ran after you and you went round again together, and then you were just going round a fourth time—"

"Wait a moment," said Winnie-the-Pooh, holding up his paw.

He sat down and thought, in the most thoughtful way he could think. Then he fitted his paw into one of the Tracks . . . and then he scratched his nose twice, and stood up.

"Yes," said Winnie-the-Pooh.

"I see now," said Winnie-the-Pooh.

"I have been Foolish and Deluded," said he, "and I am a Bear of No Brain at All."

"You're the Best Bear in All the World," said Christopher Robin soothingly.

"It seems to me that it was a reasonable mistake to make," said The Stranger.

"Really?" said Pooh, brightening up. "But anyway, that was the end of the tracking story. Does it help—with measurement, that is?"

"It certainly does. It supplies me with just the word that I need to describe much of the information many managers and workers receive.

"You see, Pooh, the first thing a manager should ask when considering measurement is: What information do I, and the others who are concerned, need to do our jobs effectively? It should be measurements and information that will enable us to direct our efforts toward desired results that we can control."

"I can see that," said Pooh. "If your job was to fill pots with honey, it wouldn't do you any good to get information that told you how many Ents you should put in each pot."

"Exactly. Yet in many organizations the measurements and information that the manager receives is similar to that. It is like you and Piglet tracking the Woozle. The information you were receiving from the paw-marks led you around in a circle and didn't really mean anything. We could call information that does that 'Woozle Measurements,' in honor of your adventure."

Pooh said "Woozle Measurements" to himself several times, just to remind himself that it was named in honor of one of his adventures. He rather liked the sound of it. Certainly having something named in honor of one of your adventures could mean you were on the verge of becoming a Very Important Bear.

"The manager must make certain that the measurements she establishes are meaningful. They must measure and provide information on what she and others really need to know. They must not be 'Woozle Measurements.'

"For instance, in many plants a manager of a department may receive the quality control results or the production figures for the plant as a whole. The workers whom she supervises get nothing. What they really need is to receive figures or measurements that show what is happening in quality and production in the manager's area of responsibility."

"Why do managers get Woozle Measurements?" asked Pooh.

"Often simply because certain measurements are already being collected, and the manager accepts that because that is the way it has always been. Often the measurements have been set up by the accounting department, for accounting department needs, which may, and usually are, very different from what a manager and her people need to know. When she asks for something different, she is often told that the figures supplied were good enough for her predecessor, so they should be good enough for her, or that the computer or the system won't allow it, or that the figures and measurements are too expensive to collect just for her.

"The manager must not accept this. She must ask herself, 'What kind of information do I and the people I am responsible for and to really need to receive in order to do our jobs properly?' Once she has decided this, then she can work out how and where to get it and what form it should be in."

"But suppose the accounting department still won't give it to her?" asked Pooh.

"Often, if you really try, you can convince them, but if not, as a last resort, the manager can collect the information herself. After all, she can't do a proper job without it. She must have it to do an excellent job, as must her people. It is not fair to them or to herself to let it slide because it is difficult to get."

"I see," said Pooh. "Are there any other rules about measurements? I like rules. They are comforting."

"Well," said The Stranger, "they should be as economical to collect as is practicable. They should be kept as simple as possible. With data processing and computers it is tempting to generate masses and masses of figures. The information may be in there somewhere in the reports, but people won't take the time to dig it out. A good principle to follow is to use exceptions. Show measurements only when they deviate from what is expected. That way you don't waste time looking at measurements that are perfectly satisfactory, and those figures that require action stand out. Charts and graphs help also.

"In addition, measurements should be timely. If you need to know something today in order to take action, it doesn't do you much good to get the measurements about it next week, when it is too late. Finally, there is the most important rule of all about measurement."

"What is that?" asked Pooh, sitting up very straight as if he were getting ready to remember it.

"Measurements must be set up by the manager so that they are used to make self-control possible. If they are used—or, I should say, abused—to control people and to dominate them, there will be a great loss of effectiveness. This is a very common situation and one that managers, if they want to be excellent managers, must guard against. It is actually the main reason why measurement is the weakest part of most managers' performance."

"I'll remember that," said Pooh, "and I think I understand better about the 'How' of measurement. Could we try measuring my honey to see if I do it properly?"

"I think that would be a very good idea," said The Stranger.

Pooh said he thought what he really needed to know was how many pots of honey he should have in his honey-cupboard to be sure to get more before he ran out. That was seven, since he liked to have a pot of honey each day, and he had always been able to get more honey within a week.

Then he counted the pots he had and got the number exactly right, which was eighteen, counting the two

small pots as one and including the three that The Stranger had brought.

He put the seven pots on the top shelf, explaining

to The Stranger that when he had used everything on the bottom two shelves, he would know it was time to go and look for some more honey.

The Stranger said he thought that was a very fine control system, which is, of course, what measurement should be used for. "There is no point in having any measurements or reports or data, unless some action is taken based on them."

"Thank you," said Pooh. "It does seem like a good system. It is ever so much less Confusing, now that I know about measurement. And since now I've got the honey properly measured and put away, can I help you to bring your picnic basket over to the table?"

VII

In WHICH Pooh, Owl, and The Stranger
Discuss the Others in the Forest to
Learn About Developing People and
Tigger is UnBounced

"It seems to me," said Pooh, "that there are two parts to it."

"Indisputably that is the case," said Owl. "Even a casual observation would reveal that there is indubitably an initial statement and then a final phrase."

"Oh," said Pooh. "I thought there were two parts to it."

"That," said Owl with dignity, "is what I said."

"I see," said Pooh. "I guess Indisputooly confused me."

Pooh had invited Owl over to his house to talk with The Stranger about the fourth function in a manager's work, that of developing people. Pooh felt that he knew less about that part of a manager's work than anything else a manager was supposed to do, and perhaps Owl's being there would help.

Owl had flown over from the Hundred Acre Wood just in time for breakfast, since he really preferred flying when the sun was not too bright. Knowing that, Pooh

had prepared for his visit by having on hand some of Owl's favorite breakfast food.

After they had finished eating,
and while they were waiting for
The Stranger, Pooh told Owl
about developing people.

"The Stranger said that a good
manager systematically works on
helping his people grow and improve and on improving
himself and his performance as a manager."

Owl nodded wisely, as if he had known that all
along, although he hadn't. Not really.

They had just decided that there were two parts to
the fourth function of a manager when Pooh's bell rang
and The Stranger came in. Owl had never met The
Stranger, so Pooh introduced them very nicely, as he
had been taught by Christopher Robin, who was learning about something called "Manners," which meant
helping elders and please and thank you and, of course,
doing introductions properly.

"I'm very pleased that you were able to come today,"
The Stranger said to Owl. "I was very impressed with
your grasp of management theories that Pooh told me
about. I'm sure you will add to today's discussion."

"Thank you," said Owl. "One does one's best, but
here in the Forest, one's opportunities for intelligent discussions about matters of moment tend to be somewhat

limited." Owl shook his head sadly from side to side. This was most impressive, since as Owl could turn his head almost all the way around, he appeared to be looking first over his right shoulder and then over his left shoulder.

"We already decided that developing people had two parts to it," said Pooh. "Owl said 'Indisputooly' that was so."

"The word," said Owl firmly, "was 'indisputably.' "

"Oh," said Pooh. "I forgot. I sometimes have difficulty with long words, although not with words like 'confuzzled' and 'expotition.' " Pooh wrinkled up his nose and scratched his head. "On the whole, I have less trouble with long 'X' words. Somehow they are easier to remember."

"If I had known that," said Owl, "I would have used an 'X' word instead. I could have said, 'Extenuating circumstances are lacking in this case.' "

"You're exactly right that there are two parts to the fourth function of a manager's job," said The Stranger. "I think we should talk about them separately."

"So we don't get Muddled," Pooh said.

"Yes. Although the objective is the same, the way a manager goes about developing his people is quite different from the way he improves himself and his performance as a manager."

"I think," said Owl, "that, if we are to have an intelligent discussion, we should say what the objective is in developing people."

"An excellent point. The objective should be to enable the individual to develop her talents and abilities to the fullest so that she can be effective in her work with the organization. Ideally, the objective is to achieve excellence within the limits of those talents and abilities and in accord with the individual's wishes."

"I see," said Owl. "Why don't we start with what the manager does to develop his people? That would be useful to know. For instance, there are some individuals here in the Forest that I think could stand some developing." And Owl named those he felt could stand some developing.

The Stranger chuckled. "I'm afraid what you have in mind, Owl, is not what we're talking about here. A manager does not try to make people over, or to change their basic personality. In the first place, I don't think that we know enough about people to be able to do that. Second, it would be deeply resented because it is manipulative and, I think, immoral."

"Still, some might profit from the process," said Owl.

"That's possible, but if we could in some way change the personality, then the individual would not be the same person. For instance, how would you describe Eeyore?"

"Eeyore is a quadruped of the horse kind but smaller, with long ears and a tuft at the end of the tail, who exhibits psychological manifestations of depression, pessimism, and occasional symptoms of a latent paranoid neurosis," said Owl.

"Eeyore is a donkey who is mostly gloomy and sad," said Pooh, "and who thinks 'They' take advantage of him and cause him problems."

"That, Pooh, is what I said," said Owl sternly.

"Oh," said Pooh. "Anyway, Eeyore is just Eeyore."

"Suppose for just a moment," said The Stranger, "that we could change Eeyore and make him like, say, Tigger, who is Bouncy and optimistic. What would you think about that?"

"You would have someone who looked like Eeyore and acted like Tigger," said Owl.

"But it wouldn't be Eeyore," said Pooh slowly. "I don't think I'd like it, and besides, one Bouncy Tigger is enough for a forest of this size. In fact," he continued, "sometimes it's almost too much. We even tried to un-Bounce Tigger once."

"Really," said The Stranger. "What happened?"

"It went something like this," said Pooh, remembering.

One day Rabbit and Piglet were sitting outside Pooh's front door listening to Rabbit, and Pooh was sitting with them. It was a drowsy summer afternoon, and the Forest was full of gentle sounds, which all seemed to be saying to Pooh, "Don't listen to Rabbit, listen to me." So he got into a comfortable position for not listening to Rabbit, and from time to time he opened his eyes to say "Ah!" and then closed them again to say "True," and from time to time Rabbit said, "You see what I mean,

Piglet," very earnestly, and Piglet nodded earnestly to show that he did.

"In fact," said Rabbit, coming to the end of it at last, "Tigger's getting so Bouncy nowadays that it's time we taught him a lesson. Don't you think so, Piglet?"

Piglet said that Tigger *was* very Bouncy, and that if they could think of a way of unbouncing him, it would be a Very Good Idea. . . .

"Well, I've got an idea," said Rabbit, "and here it is. We take Tigger for a long explore, somewhere where he's never been, and we lose him there, and next morning we find him again, and—mark my words—he'll be a different Tigger altogether."

"Why?" said Pooh.

"Because he'll be a Humble Tigger. Because he'll be a Sad Tigger, a Melancholy Tigger, a Small and Sorry Tigger, and Oh-Rabbit-I-*am*-glad-to-see-you Tigger. That's why."

"Will he be glad to see me and Piglet, too?"

"Of course."

"That's good," said Pooh.

"I should hate him to go *on* being Sad," said Piglet doubtfully.

"Tiggers never go on being Sad," explained Rabbit. "They get over it with Astonishing Rapidity. I asked Owl, just to make sure, and he said that that's what they always get over it with. But if we can make Tigger feel Small and Sad just for five minutes, we shall have done a good deed."

"Did you decide to go ahead with Rabbit's plan to change Tigger?" asked The Stranger.

"Yes, the very next day."

The next day was quite a different day. Instead of being hot and sunny, it was cold and misty. Pooh didn't mind for himself, but when he thought of all the honey the bees wouldn't be making, a cold and misty day always made him feel sorry for them. He said so to Piglet when Piglet came to fetch him, and Piglet said that he wasn't thinking of that so much, but of how cold and miserable it would be being lost all day and night on the top of the Forest. But when he and Pooh had got to Rabbit's house, Rabbit said it was just the day for them, because Tigger always bounced on ahead of everybody, and as soon as he got out of sight, they would hurry away in the other direction, and he would never see them again.

"Not never?" said Piglet.

"Well, not until we find him again, Piglet. Tomorrow, or whenever it is. Come on. He's waiting for us. . . ."

So they went. At first Pooh and Rabbit and Piglet walked together, and Tigger ran round them in circles, and then, when the path got narrower, Rabbit, Piglet and Pooh walked one after another, and Tigger ran round them in oblongs, and by-and-by, when the gorse got very prickly on each side of the path, Tigger ran up and down in front of them, and sometimes he bounced into Rabbit and sometimes he didn't. And as they got higher, the mist got thicker, so that Tigger kept disappearing, and then when you thought he wasn't there, there he was again, saying "I say, come on," and before you could say anything, there he wasn't.

Rabbit turned round and nudged Piglet.

"The next time," he said. "Tell Pooh."

"The next time," said Piglet to Pooh.

"The next what?" said Pooh to Piglet.

Tigger appeared suddenly, bounced into Rabbit, and disappeared again. "Now!" said Rabbit. He jumped into a hollow by the side of the path, and Pooh and Piglet jumped after him. They crouched in the bracken, listening. The Forest was very silent when you stopped and listened to it. They could see nothing and hear nothing. . . .

There was a moment's silence, and then they heard him pattering off

again. For a little longer they waited, until the Forest had become so still that it almost frightened them, and then Rabbit got up and stretched himself.

"Well?" he whispered proudly. "There we are! Just as I said."

"So you got Tigger lost," said The Stranger.

"Not exactly," said Pooh. "What we didn't know was that it's a funny thing about Tiggers, they never get lost.

"Nobody knows why. They just don't. So when he couldn't find us, Tigger went right back to Kanga's and started playing with Roo. They were playing the game of throwing fir cones at each other." Pooh paused. "In case you wanted to know what they were doing."

"So you found him there, when you and Piglet and Rabbit got back," said Owl.

"Not really," said Pooh. "It went more like this."

"The fact is," said Rabbit, "we've missed our way somehow."

They were having a rest in a small sand-pit on the top of the Forest. Pooh was getting rather tired of that sand-pit, and suspected it of following them about, because whichever direction they started in, they always ended up at it, and each time, as it came through the mist at them, Rabbit said triumphantly, "Now I know where we are!" and Pooh said sadly, "So do I," and Piglet said nothing. He had tried to think of something to say, but the only thing he could think of was, "Help, help!"

and it seemed silly to say that, when he had Pooh and Rabbit with him.

"Well," said Rabbit, after a long silence in which nobody thanked him for the nice walk they were having, "we'd better get on, I suppose. Which way shall we try?"

"How would it be," said Pooh slowly, "if, as soon as we're out of sight of this Pit, we try to find it again?"

"What's the good of that?" said Rabbit.

"Well," said Pooh, "we keep looking for Home and not finding it, so I thought that if we looked for this Pit, we'd be sure not to find it, which would be a Good Thing, because then we might find something that we *weren't* looking for, which might be just what we *were* looking for, really."

"So you were lost," said The Stranger.

"Well," said Pooh. "We knew where we were, and I suppose if you know where you are, you can't very well be lost. What we didn't know was where home was."

"I assume," said Owl, "that since you are here, you eventually found where home was."

"Sort of," said Pooh. "Christopher Robin came looking and found Piglet and me and took us home and we all had a little something."

"What happened to Rabbit?" asked The Stranger.

"He had gotten separated from us and was lost, but we didn't worry because Christopher Robin said he expected that Tigger would find him since he was sort of looking for us all."

Tigger was tearing round the Forest making loud yapping noises for Rabbit. And at last a very Small and Sorry Rabbit heard him. And the Small and Sorry Rabbit rushed through the mist at the noise, and it suddenly turned into Tigger; a Friendly Tigger, a Grand Tigger, a Large and Helpful Tigger, a Tigger who bounced, if he bounced at all, in just the beautiful way a Tigger ought to bounce.

"Oh, Tigger, I *am* glad to see you," cried Rabbit.

"So the adventure ended happily," said The Stranger, "but Tigger wasn't changed. He was still Bouncy."

"Yes," said Pooh. "After that, though, nobody much minded. Especially Rabbit."

"It is very, very difficult to change someone," said The Stranger, "as we said earlier. In addition, even if we could, we would probably prefer the person the way he was, as your story shows."

"But if you can't change people," asked Owl, "how does the manager carry out her responsibility of developing people?"

"That's the funny thing about this function of a manager. You see, the manager really can't develop people. It just can't be done. All she can do is to provide an environment that encourages them to develop themselves."

" 'Hows' are difficult," said Pooh, slowly shaking his head from side to side. "This seems the most difficult 'How' of all. The manager has to develop her people, but you can't develop people."

"She can't do it directly, but there is a great deal she can do indirectly. First she must know her people. She should talk to them, observe them, and, above all, listen to them. By doing that, she will begin to learn their strengths and weaknesses.

"Once she knows those, she can start to work with the individuals. She can give assignments to them, delegate some of her own work, for instance, where their strengths will help them to perform well.

"In the process, their weaknesses will show up. They will make mistakes. However, and this is extremely important, the manager should emphasize their strengths and view their mistakes in a positive way, pointing out that mistakes are a natural part of the learning experience.

"Working under these conditions, most people will want to correct their weaknesses and will work hard to do so. The important thing is that it is done on their own, not imposed from outside. No one likes to have someone continually pointing out their weaknesses."

"What else can the manager do?" asked Pooh.

"She should select her people carefully and give them work to do that will meet their needs and that is compatible with their talents, experience, and ability. She also can provide them with appropriate training if they want to take it to upgrade their skills.

"Above all, she should leave them alone. Get out of the way and let them get on with the job. Guide them, help them, but don't sit on them or smother them."

"I sat on Piglet once," said Pooh. "By accident. He didn't much care for it."

"Few do," said Owl.

"That's exactly right," said The Stranger. "Few of us like to be hovered over. By letting her people alone, unless they need help, the manager is showing that she trusts them and considers them to be competent, mature individuals. Not everyone will respond to that, but enough of any manager's people will react favorably so that a very effective operation will be possible.

"Remember that the manager's objective is for each individual to achieve excellence within the limits of his or her talents and abilities. Once the manager makes it plain that excellence is the objective, her people will strive for it themselves. Everyone likes to be a winner, and most people like to be challenged—as long as the challenge is seen to be achievable."

"Is there any more?" asked Pooh. "Or is it lunchtime?"

"There is one other thing that we should stress. The key word in our definition of the function of developing people is 'systematically.' Since the manager is attempting to reach her objective by establishing an environment or a climate that encourages growth and improvement of the individual, she must make certain that her efforts are consistent and continuous."

"I can see that," said Owl. "If the manager's efforts

are sporadic, the ambiance will be one of change and uncertainty, obviating the idea of a consistent condition surrounding and effecting the development of an organism, namely, the individual."

"What?" said Pooh, and even The Stranger had to think about what Owl had said for a few moments.

"That's exactly right, Owl," The Stranger said finally. "Growing and improving is a process that takes place over a long period of time. The individuals must know that their efforts will be rewarded at the end of that time. The environment that will do that must be a stable one that they can count on.

"And speaking of rewards, the manager should compliment individuals, preferably in public, when they do a good job in terms of their talents and abilities. Raises and promotions come along relatively infrequently, but the opportunity to congratulate someone on doing something well occurs almost daily. The manager should seize every opportunity. The compliments will reinforce her commitment to growth and encourage the individual."

"What about the manager?" asked Pooh. "She was supposed to grow and improve her performance also."

"That's a little easier," said The Stranger. "She has control over that herself. Ideally, her superior will be doing the same thing the manager is doing with her people, but even if he does not, the manager can take on the job herself. In fact, it is vital that she do so. Do you know why?"

Pooh thought for a moment. "Because," he said slowly, "when . . . we . . . were . . . talking . . . about . . . communication, we agreed that actions speak louder than words," he finished in a rush.

"Precisely. By making efforts to grow and improve her own performance, she shows her people that she considers it to be important, which also helps to create a consistent environment. Very good, Pooh."

"I try," said Pooh modestly. "But how does the manager do it for herself?"

"First, she monitors her own performance so that she can see where she needs improvement. I think one of the best ways I've found is that used by Benjamin Franklin. In his autobiography, he tells about how he decided what qualities and skills he needed in order to become successful. He made up a checklist showing each one. Then, at the end of each day, he would review the list and give himself a mark on how well he had done that day on each item. By doing this, he not only kept reminding himself what was important, he also had a running record of his progress. I've found it very helpful, and it only takes about five minutes at the end of the day."

"Is that what you meant by 'systematically'?" asked Pooh.

"Yes. In addition, the manager should decide what skills and characteristics she might need in the future and begin to learn and practice those. Often she can get an idea as to what these should be by observing and talking to her superior. She can take extension courses, and she also can volunteer for duties that her superior does and ask that they be delegated to her."

"So the manager improves her performance on the job she is doing at the present time," said Owl, "and at the same time prepares herself for her future responsibilities."

"Exactly," said The Stranger. He looked up at the sun. "Do you know, I think we've almost gone through lunchtime."

"I know," said Pooh. "My stomach told me."

VIII

In which Pooh and The Stranger Talk About the Horrible Heffalump Trap for Managers and What They Can Do to Avoid Falling into It

While Pooh, Owl, and The Stranger were eating lunch, the weather had changed. The sun was covered by clouds, and it grew quite dark outside Pooh's house. The wind blew harder and whistled in through the crack in the door, bringing with it the scent of rain.

"I think," said Owl, licking off the last bits of bread and honey that The Stranger had thoughtfully brought, "that it might well be an auspicious time for me to return to my abode before atmospheric conditions deteriorate still further."

Pooh suggested to Owl that he had better think about going home, because it looked as if it might rain.

The Stranger looked out the door and said that it looked as if it were raining already in the direction he needed to go, so if Pooh didn't mind, he'd stay around for a little while to see if the rain would pass by.

Pooh said he didn't mind at all, as he had some questions he wanted to ask.

While Pooh cleaned up after lunch, carefully leaving out the remaining little snacks from the picnic basket, he thought about the questions he wanted to ask The Stranger, who was taking a few winks in Pooh's most comfortable chair in front of the toasty fire.

The Stranger woke up just as Pooh was finishing.

"It seems to me," Pooh said, "that a manager has ever so much to do, what with Establishing Objectives and Organizing and all the rest, that I don't see how it all gets done."

The Stranger chuckled. "I'm sure most managers would agree with you. It is a big job, and the only way that someone can do it well is to be as effective as possible."

"What's 'defective'? Is that someone who works for the police? Christopher Robin once read a book about a—a—a one of those."

"You're thinking about 'detective'—someone who investigates crime. The word I used was 'effective.' It simply means that the manager must get the right things done."

Pooh thought for a minute. Finally he said, "I see. If the manager isn't getting the right things done, then he must be getting the wrong things done, and if he gets the wrong things done, then the manager won't be making progress toward achieving his objectives. That seems simple, I think."

"That's exactly right, Pooh, but you would be surprised how often managers concentrate on the wrong things simply because they haven't thought about being effective. Many managers let themselves get distracted by tasks that will not make a major contribution toward achieving their objectives and then complain because they do not have enough time to do the important things.

"A manager should always remember what he is trying to achieve and what tasks are really important in reaching his goals. Then he should concentrate on those tasks."

"It's not always easy not to be distracted," said Pooh. "Sometimes things happen. Like the time that Piglet and I were searching for Small, one of Rabbit's friends-and-relations who was lost."

"What happened to distract you?" asked The Stranger.

"Well, it all started when Rabbit told me that Small had disappeared and that everyone had been Organized into a Search. I was to search by the Six Pine Trees first and then work my way back to Owl's House where Rabbit would meet me."

As soon as Rabbit was out of sight, Pooh remembered that he had forgotten to ask who Small was, and whether he was the sort of friend-and-relation who settled on one's nose, or the sort who got trodden on by mistake, and as it was Too Late Now, he thought he would begin the Hunt by looking for Piglet, and asking him what they were looking for before he looked for it.

"That seems wise," commented The Stranger.

"I thought so. It's ever so helpful to know what you are looking for if you are looking for something. It helps you to recognize it when you find it. I even made up a list of How I should go about it."

ORDER OF LOOKING FOR THINGS

1. **Special Place.** *(To find Piglet.)*
2. **Piglet.** *(To find who Small is.)*
3. **Small.** *(To find Small.)*
4. **Rabbit.** *(To tell him I've found Small.)*
5. **Small Again.** *(To tell him I've found Rabbit.)*

"That's a good habit for a manager to acquire," said The Stranger.

"Yes," said Pooh, "probably most V.I.B.s keep lists. I was so busy writing this down in my head and not looking where I was going that I got distracted."

"Did someone interrupt you?" asked The Stranger.

"No," said Pooh. "It happened like this."

The next moment the day became very bothering indeed, because Pooh was so busy not looking where he

was going that he stepped on a piece of the Forest which
had been left out by mistake; and he only just had time
to think to himself: "I'm flying. What Owl does. I wonder how you stop—" when he stopped.

Bump!

"Ow!" squeaked something.

"That's funny," thought Pooh. "I said 'Ow!' without
really oo'ing."

"Help!" said a small, high voice.

"That's me again," thought Pooh. "I've had an Accident, and fallen down a well, and my voice has gone all
squeaky and works before I'm ready for it, because I've
done something to myself inside. Bother!"

"Help—help!"

"There you are! I say things when I'm not trying. So
it must be a very bad Accident." And then he thought
that perhaps when he did try to say things he wouldn't

be able to; so, to make sure, he said loudly: "A Very Bad Accident to Pooh Bear."

"Pooh!" squeaked the voice.

"It's Piglet!" cried Pooh eagerly. "Where are you?"

"Underneath," said Piglet in an underneath sort of way.

"Underneath what?"

"You," squeaked Piglet. "Get up! . . ."

"What's happened?" said Pooh. "Where are we?"

"I think we're in a sort of Pit. I was walking along, looking for somebody, and then suddenly I wasn't any more, and just when I got up to see where I was, something fell on me. And it was you."

"So it was," said Pooh.

"Yes," said Piglet. "Pooh," he went on nervously, and came a little closer, "do you think we're in a trap?"

Pooh hadn't thought about it at all, but now he nodded. For suddenly he remembered how he and Piglet had once made a Pooh Trap for Heffalumps, and he guessed what had happened. He and Piglet had fallen into a Heffalump Trap for Poohs! That was what it was.

"I can see where that would be distracting," said The Stranger.

"It was," said Pooh. "Very. We spent a great deal of time Not Searching for Small because we were trying to decide what to do when the Horrible Heffalump came by to inspect his Trap for Poohs and found us in it."

"What happened when the Heffalump did find you in its Trap?"

"It didn't."

Christopher Robin, who was thinking of something else, said: "Where's Pooh?"—but Rabbit had gone. So he went into his house and drew a picture of Pooh going a long walk at about seven o'clock in the morning, and then he climbed to the top of his tree and climbed down again, and then he wondered what Pooh was doing, and went across the Forest to see.

It was not long before he came to the Gravel Pit, and he looked down, and there were Pooh and Piglet, with their backs to him, dreaming happily. . . .

"Hallo, Pooh."

Piglet looked up, and looked away again. And he felt so Foolish and Uncomfortable that he had almost decided to run away to Sea and be a Sailor . . .

"So all the time you and Piglet spent deciding what to do when the Heffalump came could have been spent on getting out of the Gravel Pit and then carrying out your Search for Small."

"Yes," said Pooh. "But we were distracted. I'm afraid I was not a Very Effective Bear."

"Still," said The Stranger, "it's a good lesson for managers. If they are to be effective, they must force themselves to set priorities and not allow themselves to be distracted. They must stay with their priority decisions. They must do first things first and second things not at all. They must be alert not to fall into the Horrible Heffalump Trap of being distracted from accomplishing their priority tasks."

"I understand that," said Pooh. "Is there anything else that a manager must do in order to be effective other than setting priorities and then sticking to them?"

"There are several. But probably the most important

thing that a manager must do in order to be effective is to manage time properly."

"How is that done?" asked Pooh, in a puzzled tone of voice. "Time just goes by. It doesn't seem to me that you can change it."

"That's very true. Everyone has the same amount of time, twenty-four hours in a day. However, some people manage to accomplish a great deal in those twenty-four hours and others very little. The reason for the difference is that those who accomplish a lot devote their time to tasks that will help them to meet their objectives—to productive tasks. They do this by eliminating or reducing as much as possible unproductive demands on their time."

"How do they do that?"

"The starting point should be for the manager to find out how he spends his time. What he is actually doing—what tasks he is performing at the present and how much time is devoted to them. He does this by keeping a record of how he spends his time each day for about a month. He records what he does as he does it and how much time it took to do it. This is called a 'Time Log,' and it is a good idea for a manager to keep one about every six months, simply because the work a manager does will change.

"The manager then can analyze his Time Log and eliminate or reduce the time spent on work that does not contribute to his priority tasks and objectives."

"How does he do that?" asked Pooh.

"Many techniques can be used. Two good books on the subject are *The Effective Executive* by Peter F. Drucker and *How to Get Control of Your Time and Your Life* by Alan Lakein.

"Finally, the manager should schedule the time available to him. A good way to do this is to sit down at a time when he will be undisturbed, say on a Sunday evening, or the first thing Monday morning, with an appointment book and think about what needs to be accomplished in the coming week.

"He should first consider his priority items and schedule blocks of time to work on them. Care must be taken not to schedule too much of the time available. If someone overschedules, he will get discouraged because he can't accomplish what was scheduled. Every manager knows that there are always interruptions and unscheduled events, so count on it in advance. Schedule only about 60 percent of the time. Leave the rest open. If nothing occurs, the manager can always rejuggle or expand the time scheduled on priority items.

"Then each day, either at the end of the day or first thing in the morning, he should review and adjust the schedule for the upcoming day and the rest of the week."

"It seems to me," said Pooh, "that the scheduling would take a lot of time, all by itself."

"Not really. After you are used to doing it, you would find that only about a half an hour is required for the weekly scheduling and about five minutes for the daily review and adjustment."

"That doesn't seem like a lot of time," said Pooh. "That's only about the amount of time in a week that I spend each day for a little afternoon snack, which normally would be scheduled right about now."

"Well," said The Stranger, walking over to the window and looking out, "a good manager doesn't deviate from the schedule unless it is absolutely necessary. The rain has passed over, and it's about time for me to be leaving. Let's have the scheduled snack and then I must be on my way."

"There are a few things left over from the picnic basket you brought. If we had them for a Little Something, then the basket would be lighter for you to carry," suggested Pooh most helpfully.

The Stranger agreed and they sat down to have a Little Something, which turned out to be a Large Something.

As they were eating The Stranger asked Pooh: "When you told me your story about the Search for Small, you never said if Small was found."

"Oh yes, I forgot. Just when Christopher Robin came along, I was trying to soothe myself in that awkward place in the middle of the back where something was tickling me when suddenly Piglet gave a shout."

"Pooh!" he cried. "There's something climbing up your back."

"I thought there was," said Pooh.
"It's Small!" cried Piglet.
"Oh, *that*'s who it is, is it?" said Pooh.
"Christopher Robin, I've found Small!" cried Piglet.
"Well done, Piglet," said Christopher Robin.

IX

In which The Stranger Comes to the Forest for the Last Time, a Party Is Held, Pooh Becomes a Very Important Bear, and an Enchanted Place Is Visited

Everyone knew that The Stranger would be visiting the Forest for the last time and that there would be a party. No one was quite sure how they knew this.

Piglet was absolutely and positively certain that he had heard it from Rabbit, and Rabbit was equally sure that Piglet had told him. Owl claimed to have picked up the news from the wind that sighed softly through the trees.

Kanga was told by Roo, who was so excited at the idea of a party that he completely forgot who had told him.

Tigger said that he just knew. "Tiggers always know about things like that," he said. "Tiggers are very good at knowing."

Pooh knew. He thought that The Stranger had told him just before he left on the day it had rained, but then again, he wasn't sure, since they had talked so much that day that his brain had gotten tired and refused to remember exactly what The Stranger had said. When he woke up the morning of the party, he lay in bed and tried to remember how he knew.

Knowing made Pooh feel sad. He liked having The Stranger visit the Forest because The Stranger treated him like a Bear of Some Brain instead of a Bear of Little Brain. He also liked the picnic baskets that The Stranger brought, or rather, what was inside the baskets.

Thinking about the picnic baskets reminded him about the party, which made him feel glad. Since The Stranger had brought such good food in the picnic baskets, the food for the party should be even better, since parties are supposed to be Special.

"Let's see now," he said to himself, since no one else was around, "there will probably be a pot, no, two pots of honey. Or will there be three?"

That was a difficult question and Pooh finally decided that the correct number was probably three.

"Then there are sure to be some of those little cake things with Pink Sugar icing. Maybe even enough so that one can have More if one is so inclined. Then for dessert there will be honeycombs that are nice and chewy and lots and lots of orange marmalade to spread on them to make them go down even easier—" and Pooh happily dreamed on.

Even Eeyore knew. "Someone must have made a mistake," he said gloomily. "Mostly no one tells me what is happening until it's Too Late. That's sad, but it's just the way things are. Probably there isn't going to be a party. I'll go and when I get there everyone will jump out and say 'Surprise!' and the surprise will be that there isn't a party after all. How like them.

"On the other hoof, if I don't go and there really is a party, I shall miss it. Still, I suppose they would be sending me down the odd bits that got trodden on. Kind and Thoughtful."

In the end, Eeyore decided to attend. He and the others got ready.
Eeyore had considerable difficulty
getting the bow on his tail tied exactly right since his tail kept acting
like it was once again thinking about
becoming a bell-pull, but in the end, he managed it.

Owl took particular care and made certain that his claws were spotless and well polished. After all, his contribution to the book The
Stranger was writing was indubitably of in-
estimable value, and it was not inconceiv-
able that the festivities were conceived to
give recognition to his preoption to in-
scribe the dedication of the tome.

Piglet actually considered washing before he went to the party. He thought about it for a long time and then decided that if he did so, it was quite likely that no one would recognize him, and he would not be allowed to attend. So he didn't. Wash, that is.

Kanga gave Roo a thorough bath, even including washing inside his ears. For once, Roo didn't splash, but sat quietly thinking about the party. When Kanga finished, there weren't even any puddles on the  floor except for one very small one that hardly counted.

Rabbit was wondering if he should invite all his friends-and-relations. The Stranger might not be expecting that many and might not have brought enough chairs.

Finally he decided that if he didn't invite them, they would probably all come anyway. They could spread themselves on the grass and wait hopefully in case anybody spoke to them, or dropped anything, or asked them the time.

While Roo was being dried off, Tigger carefully groomed himself, licking his fur until it all lay down in exactly the right place and shone silkily in the sunlight. Tigger admired himself in the mirror after he had finished, commenting "Tiggers are very good at looking well groomed."

Pooh, deciding he had dreamed about the food that would be at the party long enough and that he had better get ready for the real thing just to see if he had dreamed it correctly, got up and carefully brushed  his fur into place. It had gotten all scrambled while he slept and didn't look at all like the Fur of a Bear Who Is Going to a Party.

Finally everyone was ready and found their way to where a long table and chairs had been set up at the base of one of the largest trees in the Forest. Even Eeyore arrived on time, saying "Don't blame me if it rains."

It didn't rain. It was, in fact, a beautiful, warm, sunny day. The earlier rains had washed everything clean, and the leaves shone as they nodded and fluttered in the soft, gentle breezes that whispered through the Forest. Little spots of sunlight danced across the food, which covered every inch of the table.

There was everything that Pooh had dreamed about and more. There was even enough so that all of Rabbit's friends-and-relations did not have to depend on What Someone Might Carelessly Drop. There were specially succulent thistles fresh cut for Eeyore, haycorns for Piglet, Extract of Malt for Tigger, and plenty of honey, bread, and condensed milk for everyone. And little cake things with Pink Sugar icing, of course.

When they all had eaten nearly enough, and then some more, The Stranger stood up and made a speech. He told them nicely how much he appreciated their contribution to his book.

"Contri—what?" asked Pooh.

"Hush," said Owl. "What you told him."

"Oh," said Pooh.

He said he was sorry to be leaving, but that he

would come back to the Forest someday. Then The Stranger thanked everyone by name, even Small, and told them He Could Not Have Done It Without Them.

Everyone clapped and then Eeyore and Owl both began to make a speech at the same time; Owl starting "Unaccustomed as I am—" and Eeyore beginning "At least it didn't rain—yet." Since each was listening only to his own speech, they both continued, which made it very difficult for those around the table to understand what either one was saying.

It didn't really matter, however, because it was a good time to have just a little smidgen more of your favorite Whatever. Pooh had two Mores of the little cake things with Pink Sugar icing.

When the Owl/Eeyore speech was over and everyone had clapped enough, Pooh stood up.

"When you first came to the Forest," he said, looking at The Stranger, "I fear I was a Bear of Very Little Brain, particularly about Management. Now I know a little about it and about what a manager should do in order to be a Good Manager. You even very carefully explained the 'Hows' so that I could understand them." Pooh shook his head. "I have always had difficulty with 'Hows.' 'Whats' are not nearly as hard."

"Tiggers are Very Good at 'Hows,'" said Tigger in a muffled, faraway-under-the-table kind of voice.

"Yes," said Pooh, wondering where Tigger had gotten to. "But I also think I understand a 'Why.' I think I understand why a manager is."

"Why is a manager?" asked The Stranger.

"It's like when I went visiting Rabbit one day after I had finished doing my Stoutness Exercises in front of the mirror. Because of Rabbit's hospitality, I ate too much." Pooh patted his stomach. "Almost as much as today, and when I tried to go home, I got stuck in Rabbit's front door, which was wide enough going in but too narrow when one wanted to come out."

"So what happened then?" asked The Stranger.

"Rabbit told me what the Trouble was."

"The fact is," said Rabbit, "you're stuck."

"It all comes," said Pooh crossly, "of not having front doors big enough."

"It all comes," said Rabbit sternly, "of eating too much. I thought at the time," said Rabbit, "only I didn't like to say anything," said Rabbit, "that one of us was eating too much," said Rabbit, "and I knew it wasn't *me*," he said. "Well, well, I shall go and fetch Christopher Robin. . . ."

Christopher Robin nodded.

"Then there's only one thing to be done," he said. "We shall have to wait for you to get thin again."

"How long does getting thin take?" asked Pooh anxiously.

"About a week, I should think."

"But I can't stay here for a *week*!"

"You can *stay* here all right, silly old Bear. It's getting you out which is so difficult."

"We'll read to you," said Rabbit cheerfully. "And I hope it won't snow," he added. "And I say, old fellow, you're taking up a good deal of room in my house—*do* you mind if I use your back legs as a towel-horse? Because, I mean, there they are—doing nothing—and it would be very convenient just to hang the towels on them."

"A week!" said Pooh gloomily. *"What about meals?"*

"I'm afraid no meals," said Christopher Robin, "because of getting thin quicker. But we *will* read to you."

Bear began to sigh, and then found he couldn't because he was so tightly stuck; and a tear rolled down his eye, as he said:

"Then would you read a Sustaining Book, such as would help and comfort a Wedged Bear in Great Tightness?"

So for a week Christopher Robin read that sort of book at the North end of Pooh, and Rabbit hung his washing on the South end . . . and in between Bear felt himself getting slenderer and slenderer. And at the end of the week Christopher Robin said, *"Now!"*

So he took hold of Pooh's front paws and Rabbit took hold of Christopher Robin, and all Rabbit's friends and relations took hold of Rabbit, and they all pulled together. . . .

And for a long time Pooh only said *"Ow!"* . . .

And *"Oh!"* . . .

And then, all of a sudden, he said *"Pop!"* just as if a cork were coming out of a bottle.

And Christopher Robin and Rabbit and all Rabbit's friends and relations went head-over-heels backwards . . . and on the top of them came Winnie-the-Pooh— free!

"And that's why a manager is," said Pooh.

"To get you out of tight places when you eat too much?" asked Eeyore.

"No," said Pooh. "To get everyone to pull together in order to accomplish an objective."

Afterward, when everyone except Pooh and The Stranger had gone home and all the cleaning up had been done, The Stranger suggested that they take a little walk to work off some of the Fullness.

They walked along, not talking very much, except things like "The pink icing was unusually good, wasn't it?" and "Everyone made good speeches, didn't they?" until at last they came to an enchanted place on the very top of the Forest called Galleons Lap where Pooh had gone once before, a long time ago, with Christopher Robin before he went away.

The place was indeed enchanted. Its floor was close-set grass, quiet and smooth and green. It was still the only place in the Forest where you could sit down care-

lessly, without getting up again almost at once and looking for someplace else.

No one could count the sixty-odd trees that surrounded the glade in a circle. Sitting there, Pooh and The Stranger could see the whole world spread out until it reached the sky.

In the enchanted place, everything seemed to be very simple and easy to understand, even management, and somehow, accomplishing anything that

one wanted to accomplish did not appear to be at all difficult.

Pooh sat quietly, his back against one of the trees, and thought about all that The Stranger and he had talked about.

"Do you think I might?" he finally asked.

"Might what, Pooh?"

"Do you think I might really become a Very Important Bear since I helped you with a Very Important Subject like Management? If your book gets published, that is."

"Pooh, in my opinion, it doesn't matter if my book gets published or not, you always have been, are, and always will be a Very, Very Important Bear."

"Oh," thought Pooh. "That sort of Bear!"

X

In which The Stranger Thinks About Visiting the Forest, What Was Found There, and What Was Brought Back

The Stranger leaned back in his comfortable armchair, which was placed at exactly the right distance from the Very Nice Fire burning on the hearth. Outside it was a rainy, blusterous sort of day that made the fire seem even cozier and caused the flames to flare up from time to time and then settle back and crackle quietly to itself.

One might, if one had to be outdoors and struggle with a turned-inside-out umbrella and cold rain trickling down the back of a neck, be inclined to say that this was not a Friendly Day. But indoors, with all your work done, a comforting fire, an easy chair, a little something from the kitchen on the table beside you, and a Very Good Book, it was a Perfect Day. A day just made to think and dream and maybe even nap a little.

The Stranger was thinking about the Forest where

Winnie-the-Pooh and his friends lived. At first glance, it seemed a far different world from our everyday one of mind-boggling change, constant crises, confrontations, insecurity, stress, and ephemeral morality.

However, that is only the way it seemed. "Pooh's world is actually much like ours," The Stranger thought. What could be more stressful than to be caught in a Horrible Heffalump Trap? Imagine the insecurity of being down to your last pot of honey with no bee-tree in sight or the unsettling change of having Strange Animals, who are generally regarded as one of the Fiercer Animals, move into your neighborhood.

Visiting the Forest, The Stranger found that their adventures could be used to illustrate and emphasize managerial skills that could be applied equally well to their problems and ours. The "Hows" of the six functions a manager needs to perform are universal: Establishing objectives; organizing; communicating; developing people; motivating; and measurement and analysis are applicable to any field of endeavor—an Expotition to the North Pole, business, the public sector, volunteer work, professions, or one's private life.

In the Forest, however, problems somehow do not seem as complex or the consequences as serious as those we face. Besides, in the Hundred Acre Wood, there is always the comforting thought that Christopher Robin will come along to set things straight if All Else Fails.

In our society, we can't always count on a Christopher Robin standing in the wings waiting to help. We need to rely on our own and our collective talents, abilities, and resources. Excellent managers are needed, and the need will be even greater in the future.

Having problems and difficulties is the nature of life and the reason we need excellent managers. Mastery of the six functions of the manager's job will not eliminate the problems, but it will ensure that on the journey through the Forest, there will be fewer gorsebushes and thistles along the way and ambushes will be encountered less frequently.

Those who strive for excellence will help us all to meet the challenges the future will bring.

"So," The Stranger thought, "we should begin now. It is never too early to start, and every single one of us can improve our performance if we really want to. There is an old Chinese saying that 'Not to advance is to fall behind.'

"Start now with Benjamin Franklin's checklist and begin to move toward excellence as a manager."

The Stranger relaxed. He was comfortable with what he had brought back from his visit to the Forest. He knew that Pooh would wish everyone well in their efforts to improve.

And, after all, what could be more conducive to success than to have on your side as guide and inspiration a V.I.B. like Winnie-the-Pooh?

Winnie-the-Pooh
on Problem Solving

To Fathers and Sons

ACKNOWLEDGMENTS

First and foremost, we should like to thank Alan Alexander Milne, and his son Christopher Robin Milne, without whose love and tenderness for each other, the world would be a bleaker place for want of a Certain Bear and his Friends.

Our thanks go out to the Milne estate for their kind approval and permission for the use of the excerpts and illustrations for this work.

We thank our editor, Matthew Carnicelli, for providing the guidance and editorial insight.

We thank our families for being there when needed and leaving us alone when isolation was required.

There are many people at Dutton that have helped create and produce this book, and while there are many we haven't met or don't know, we would like to thank

Joan Powers, PhD (Doctor of Poohology), Lisa Johnson and the entire Publicity department for their efforts on our behalf, especially Kate Cambridge, our publicist, and all the others who have lent their efforts.

CONTENTS

INTRODUCTION

Not so very long ago a book was published which was called *Winnie-the-Pooh on Management: In which a Very Important Bear and his friends are introduced to a Very Important Subject.* (My, that is a very long title.)

Because some people read the book and some ever so kindly said they liked it and because there was more to say, it was decided to do another book. This one, that is.

This book is about how to solve problems. In the sense that solving problems is something that a manager often does and should be really good at doing, this book *could* be considered to be a continuation of *Winnie-the-Pooh on Management In which, etc., etc., etc.* However, this *is* a book for *everybody*, including managers.

You see, everyone has or will have problems. Success and/or happiness (defined however you like) depend to a considerable extent upon how well you solve the problems you take on and those that life presents to you.

The problem is, many people have problems with problems. Sometimes they don't solve a problem in the best way and end up with more problems or more serious problems. Many times they are not certain just how to solve the problem, where to start, or even what to do. As a result they do nothing, suffer the consequences of not solving it, or else limit their potential unnecessarily.

So, wouldn't it be great if there were a routine, easy way that problems could almost always be solved? A way that showed you where to start and step-by-step what to do? A way to solve a problem or improve a situation that you feel is less than satisfactory?

As you may have guessed, there *is* a way. We use it routinely in our consulting work (which consists for the most part of solving other people's problems). We think it is one of the most helpful things we know and use, in both our work and our personal lives, and we thought it would be a good thing to share.

So that is why this book was written.

Now, before we go any further, there are a few things we would like to explain for those who haven't read *Winnie-the-Pooh on Management In which etc.*, *etc.*, *etc.* (and you needn't have read it first to benefit from this book).

First, the adventures of Winnie-the-Pooh and friends (who very nicely gave us permission) were used because in our consulting work we found that people learned more easily and remembered better what was taught when we used their adventures. Much better than if we said, "This is the way Microsoft or McDonald's does it." Or, "This is how successful people do it." Psychologists call this technique placing material to be learned in an unfamiliar context. For instance, which is easier to remember? A weather forecaster saying, "The cumulative effect of atmospheric disturbances, fluctuating lows and highs, and the overall effect of the El Niño current will tend to result in alternating periods of precipitation and no precipitation," or the gloomy Eeyore observing, "Sometimes it rains and sometimes it doesn't. That's just the way it is."

Second, in *Winnie-the-Pooh on Management In which etc., etc., etc.*, Pooh meets The Stranger in the Hundred Acre Wood. The Stranger asks Pooh's help in writing a book about management basics. He is called "The Stranger" because that was the name Pooh thought of at the time, and it stuck even though it wasn't his real name. It is used again in this book because it is still sticking. As Winnie-the-Pooh, whose real name is Edward Bear, would say, "Some have nicknames and some haven't and there it is."

Finally, we thought we should have a shorter title for this book than you-know-what. It is our belief that a good title should tell someone standing in front of a book what the book is about. So *Winnie-the-Pooh on Problem Solving* was a logical choice.

When we had gotten to this point, Piglet looked up and complained that this book wasn't about him.

We told him that he was in the whole book and it *was* about him.

"So it is about Pooh," he squeaked. You see what it is. He is jealous because he thinks Pooh is having a Grand Introduction all to himself. Pooh is the favourite, of course, there's no denying it, but Piglet comes in for a good many things which Pooh misses: because you can't take Pooh to school without everybody knowing it, but Piglet is so small that he slips into a pocket, where it is very comfortable to feel him when you are not quite sure whether twice seven is twelve or twenty-two. Sometimes he slips out and has a good look in the ink-pot, and in this way he has got more education than Pooh, but Pooh doesn't mind. Some have brains, and some haven't he says, and there it is.

While we were explaining all this to Piglet, we were typing, and when we had finished we showed him the title of this book:

"Winnie-the-Pooh on Problem Solving In which Pooh, Piglet, and friends explore How to Solve Problems, so you can too." Which, although it isn't any shorter than *Winnie-the-Pooh on Management In which etc., etc., etc.,* does tell what the book is about.

"There's my name!" Piglet squeaked excitedly. "So the book *is* about me!"

This shows the value of an education—you can recognize your own name, especially when it is in the title of a book.

And now that we have solved Piglet's problem, we should stop writing introductions and get on with the book.

I

IN WHICH Winnie-the-Pooh Hosts a Gathering, The Stranger Returns to the Forest, and Almost Everyone Is Introduced to the SOLVE Problem-Solving Method

Everybody goes to Pooh's and almost everyone was at Pooh's. Of course, Christopher Robin was not and, as usual, Alexander Beetle was missing. Kanga had sent her regrets, but Tigger had brought Roo. Some of Rabbit's friends-and-relations may not have been there, but there were so many of them no one was really sure if they were or weren't. Piglet was particularly pleased that Small, who was one of the few individuals smaller than he was, had arrived riding on Eeyore's back.

Early that morning, Owl had swooped down from the sky to tell Pooh that he (Owl) had seen The Stranger getting off the train at the station in the village.

"Indisputably The Stranger is honoring the commitment he elucidated on the occasion of his departure to rendezvous with us at some indeterminate point in the future," Owl had explained.

"Oh," said Pooh as though he had understood what Owl said.

"He is walking in this direction and is carrying two large hampers," Owl added.

"Oh." Pooh understood that. "Two *large* hampers you say."

"Yes," said Owl. "If you agree, I'll go tell the others to come here to welcome The Stranger."

Pooh agreed that was a good idea, and began Straightening Things Up as Owl flew off. He paid particular attention to making certain that there was space on the larder shelves just in case The Stranger needed to leave whatever was left over from the large hampers at Pooh's. The last time The Stranger visited, he had brought honey, so Pooh had a particular interest in clearing his larder.

The Stranger came just after the last of the others had arrived, and Pooh was glad that Owl had been right. They were two *very* large hampers that The Stranger placed on the table.

Everyone's greetings and Hallos were made. Pooh made a very nice welcoming speech. When he had finished, The Stranger said he wanted to talk to them and ask them all a favor.

"There is a new book that I'm working on and I would like to ask you if I could use your adventures in writing it as I did with *Winnie-the-Pooh on Management*."

"What is it about?" Pooh asked. He was hoping that it might have been about management like the other book, which had said he was a V.I.B. (Very Important Bear).

"It's about Problem Solving."

"Prob . . . lem Solv . . . ing?" Pooh said slowly, scratching his head. "That sounds like a 'What.' 'Whats' are easy. It's the 'Hows' that are difficult. Will it be about the 'Hows' also?"

"Yes, Pooh," The Stranger answered. "It will show how almost anybody can become very good at finding solutions to problems or improving things."

"Even me?" squeaked Piglet. "I'm really not very good at solving problems. Often when there is a problem I get a headache or I try to go home. If I can, that is. With some problems you can't, you know. Like when Kanga thinks you are Roo and washes you and makes you take strengthening medicine."

Roo giggled. Piglet frowned to show that he didn't think that was very funny. Getting washed was a very serious subject and changed your color besides.

"Certainly, Piglet," The Stranger continued. "The book will teach a routine, easy way that anyone can use to solve problems or improve a situation. If any of you here in the forest would like to learn, you could do it while I'm working on the book."

"Is it important to know how to solve problems?" asked Pooh. He liked the idea of being a Very Important Bear, and if solving problems was important maybe it would help if he learned how. To solve problems that is.

"Very important. And it is becoming more and more so. Because of change and technology there are many new problems that need to be solved, that we've never had to solve before. That can be difficult because we can't say, 'Oh, that's just the same problem we solved last year.' We have to solve them without the benefit of experience. Examples of those would be the ones in the computer field and in communications and the Internet and DNA and—"

"That sounds about what one might expect," Eeyore interrupted. "Change almost always causes problems. I can remember when my house moved from one side of the pinewood to the other. It was very upsetting. Especially when I didn't know where it had moved to and it was snowing."

"We don't have much to do with things like ABC's and nets and things here in the Forest," said Rabbit. "Would this still help us?"

"Yes," said The Stranger. "This book will help with any kind of problem, old or new." The Stranger looked around the room. "May I use your adventures, and would you like to learn while I'm working on the book?"

"Yes," and "I'd like that," said Pooh and Piglet together. The others talked about whether it would be worth learning or not learning because once they solved their problems what could they use it for. Eeyore pointed out that it was unlikely that there would be a shortage of problems even if they all got very good at solving them. They all agreed that The Stranger should go ahead.

After he had thanked them, The Stranger said that if they didn't mind, he would like to get started and at least give them an idea about Problem Solving before they stopped for lunch.

Pooh minded, but since no one else said anything, he kept quiet.

"Well . . ." The Stranger began.

"I thought this was going to be about Problem Solving, not a hole in the ground," said Eeyore gloomily. "I might have known that I'd get it wrong."

"No, Eeyore," said The Stranger. "You didn't get it wrong. I just said 'Well' as a way to begin."

"Beginnings are almost always difficult," commented Pooh, frowning. "Sometimes beginnings start before you are ready for them and that can be a problem."

"Tiggers like solving problems," Tigger said cheerfully. "They are very good at it." Tigger looked thoughtful. "What *is* a problem?" he asked.

"That's a very good place to begin, Tigger," said The Stranger. "We'll start by talking about what a problem is."

Tigger bounced up and down three times, upsetting Piglet, who didn't like to be bounced on. "See," said Tigger. "Tiggers are good at this."

Piglet whispered something about extreme bounciness being considered a problem, especially when done by certain striped individuals, but Tigger didn't hear him.

"If we look at a dictionary," The Stranger continued, "we find that a problem is defined as 'a question proposed for a solution' and as 'a perplexing or difficult matter, person, or thing.' Can any of you give me an example of a problem?"

"Bounciness," said Piglet firmly. Louder this time.

"A tail that wants to be a bell pull," Eeyore added. "No sense of its proper place in life."

"How do you get honey from a Bee Tree?" Pooh said quickly, not wanting to be left out and also really wanting to know the solution. "That's a question proposed for a solution and it's also a perplexing and difficult matter if the bees don't want you to have it."

"Very good!" The Stranger beamed. "You've given three examples of very different problems. What is even better is that they can be used to point out one of the problems with problems and why so many individuals have difficulty solving the problems they encounter.

"You see, because problems often seem to be very different, it is natural to think that each one must be solved in a different way, and this really isn't the case at all."

"It isn't?" asked Owl, making certain that he was following the discussion. As he often said, the only problem with living in the Forest was that there was not much opportunity for intelligent discussions.

"No," The Stranger continued. "Over the years, ways have been developed to deal with problems using the same approach no matter how different the problems may be. These are called Problem-Solving Methods. Some of them have as many as ten steps, but the one we will use is one that was developed to be short, easy to use, and simple to remember. It is a five-step procedure called the SOLVE Problem-Solving Method."

"I don't understand," said Pooh slowly. "How does taking five steps solve the problem of say—ah—getting honey from the Bee Tree? In what direction do you take the steps?"

"It is inherently obvious that he is not referring to a numerical progression of ambulation, but rather to a number of actions that should be accomplished in a prescribed manner so as to effectively attack something that is bothersome with the objective of situational improvement or elimination," Owl explained.

"Oh," said Pooh, who didn't really understand anything that Owl had said, except the word "bothersome."

"Owl is correct," said The Stranger. "Putting it another way, we could say that the Problem-Solving Method is a list of things we should do in order to solve problems. What we should do first and what next and so on until we have solved the problem."

"Do you call it the SOLVE Method because it helps you to find the solutions to problems?" asked Owl, who was enjoying participating in the discussion and wanted to be certain he was holding up his end.

The Stranger nodded. "Partly for that reason, but also because it is an acronym for the steps that we follow in solving any problem."

Owl blinked his eyes and looked wise, which was very easy for him to do. He just wasn't sure what The Stranger had said SOLVE was. It had sounded as though he had said "A crow limb," but somehow Owl didn't think that was what he meant.

"What's an acro—acro—acro, what you said?" asked Roo, speaking up for the first time.

Since Roo was very young, everyone felt it was perfectly all right for him to ask the question. They all waited for the answer.

The Stranger looked pleased. "*Very* good, Roo," he said. "If there is something that you don't know or don't understand, always ask. Don't be afraid that others might think that you are not very smart. They might think that or make fun of you, but the fact that you asked shows that you are really intelligent."

"I was just about to ask," said Pooh, "but he beat me to it."

"Me too!" squeaked Piglet.

"I'm glad to hear that," The Stranger continued. "An acronym is a word formed from the first letters of several words. It is used so that you don't have to say all the words each time, and it is also a way to remind us what the words are that it stands for."

"So SOLVE really means something else," said Eeyore. "You might know. Anything to throw one off."

"Each letter of SOLVE stands for one of the steps that we need to take in order to solve a problem." The Stranger thought for a moment. "It is like going around in a circle.

"There is a problem, so you need or want to solve it.

Thinking of that reminds you of SOLVE, which in turn tells you exactly what you should do first and next and next until you find the solution."

"I think I see," said Pooh. "But I might understand it better if I knew what the words were that SOLVE stands for."

"I'll give them to you, but they won't mean much until we have had a chance to explain them in detail. However, we might as well start to learn them. In fact, I think I'll write them down." The Stranger walked over to the hampers he had brought, opened one, and took out a large tablet, an easel, and a pen.

Pooh was rather disappointed to see him do this because he had thought that the hampers were only for food. While The Stranger was setting up the easel along the wall where everyone could see it, Pooh peeked in the half-open basket and was relieved to see that it was still almost full of food.

"I'll write this down in the way that you will want to remember it," said The Stranger. This is what he wrote:

S elect the Problem or Situation.
O bserve, Organize, and Define the Problem or Situation.
L earn by Questioning All Parts of the Problem.
V isualize Possible Solutions, Select One, and Refine It.
E mploy the Solution and Monitor Results.

They all looked at it and then Piglet, who, except for The Stranger and Owl, was probably the best reader there, because of the many times he had gone to school in Christopher Robin's pocket, jumped up and down, squeaking, "Look! Look! If you read down only the first letter of each line you get S-O-L-V-E. That's SOLVE."

"Indisputally," said Owl, peering closely at what was written on the tablet. "I would venture to make the assumption that the remainder of the writing enscripted there comprises the steps that should be followed."

"Very good, Owl," said The Stranger. "You are exactly right."

"I think I understand the SOLVE idea," said Pooh. "But I don't understand the rest of it. I fear I am a Bear of Little Brain."

"Not at all," said The Stranger. "It's just that I haven't explained it yet. I promise you that you'll understand it when we use some of your adventures to make it clear."

"Oh," said Pooh, feeling somewhat better.

"First, however," The Stranger said, "it seems to me that it must be lunchtime. I think we'll learn better if we have a little something to eat before we continue."

"Oh, yes!" said Pooh, feeling much, much better.

The Stranger unpacked one of the hampers and put the food out on the table. "Pooh," he said, "since it is your house, why don't you start? Would you like to begin with some condensed milk or would you prefer honey?"

Pooh stood there, thinking about it.

Piglet, who had lined up behind him and was waiting for him to make up his mind, said, "That's a problem. You might even call it a Pooh-plexing problem. We might use that for a sample problem to use SOLVE on. After lunch, that is."

"No," said Pooh. "I've solved it. I'll start with both."

II

In which the Nature of Problems Is Explored and Tigger's, Rabbit's, and Piglet's Adventures Are Used As Examples

Lunch was over and Pooh had finished checking the hamper to make sure that there was nothing left that should be eaten so it wouldn't spoil. Everyone had helped in the cleaning up.

Pooh remembered that The Stranger had said that after lunch they would Explore and Explain just what problems were and were not.

Pooh felt very good about that because if there was anything in the way of words that were easy, it was X words. All you had to do was to find two straight sticks the same size in the Forest and put one on top of the other. Then you moved them around until they looked like an X. There wasn't much chance that it would be Wobbly. Then you added the rest of the word. If you cared to, that is.

Pooh settled down not too near the fireplace. Sitting too close tended to make him sleepy if he had just eaten.

The Stranger started to talk. "Does everyone remember what we decided a problem was?"

Everyone nodded and Owl spoke up. "We decided that it is a query propounded for exegesis culminating in a verbal expression of 'Eureka.' "

Pooh rather liked that and wished he had said it because it had two X words in it.

"Everything," said Eeyore gloomily. "But a tail is especially a problem. One that doesn't stay in its proper place."

"Very good," said The Stranger. "Remember that the dictionary defined a problem as 'A question proposed for a solution,' just—"

"That is precisely what I elucidated," interrupted Owl, looking sternly at The Stranger.

"Indeed it is," said The Stranger. "I was going to say . . . 'just as Owl said.' Very good, Owl."

"Oh," said Owl. "Thank you. One does try, you know."

Pooh wondered what had happened to 'Exegesis' but didn't get a chance to ask before The Stranger continued.

"My dictionary also defined a problem as 'a difficult matter, person, or thing' . . ."

"Just what I said," muttered Eeyore. " 'Everything' covers all that, you know. But do you think I'd get credit? Not very likely. But there you are."

". . . which is what Eeyore's 'everything' implied," finished The Stranger.

"Credit where credit is due," said Eeyore. "Better late than never, I suppose."

"Now that we have reviewed what a problem is," The Stranger continued, "let's see what we can learn about the nature of problems. Pooh, before lunch you said getting honey was a problem."

"Yes," said Pooh, and just in case The Stranger was going to solve it right now, he added, "Getting honey, and getting enough, every time. Which is often."

The Stranger turned to Tigger. "Is getting honey a problem for you?" he asked.

Tigger thought for a moment. "No." He shook his head and his tail at the same time just to lend emphasis to his answer. Tiggers are very good at doing that.

"Why do you say that?" asked The Stranger.

"Because I remember when I first came to the Forest, I went to Pooh's house. It was the middle of the night and Pooh heard me, got out of bed, and opened his front door."

"I thought he might be a Strange Animal," said Pooh. "Making a noise of some kind. I got up to ask him not to do it."

"I remember that," said The Stranger. "Here it is in the book I brought along. I'll read it."

"Hallo!" said Pooh, in case there was anything outside.

"Hallo!" said Whatever-it-was.

"Oh!" said Pooh. "Hallo!"

"Hallo!"

"Oh *there* you are!" said Pooh. "Hallo!"

"Hallo!" said the Strange Animal, wondering how long this was going on.

Pooh was just going to say "Hallo" for the fourth time when he thought he wouldn't, so he said: "Who is it?" instead.

"Me," said a voice.

"Oh!" said Pooh. "Well, come here."

So Whatever-it-was came here and in the light of the candle he and Pooh looked at each other.

"I'm Pooh," said Pooh.

"I'm Tigger," said Tigger.

"Oh!" said Pooh, for he had never seen an animal like this before. "Does Christopher Robin know about you?"

"Of course he does," said Tigger.

"Well," said Pooh, "it's the middle of the night, which is a good time for going to sleep. And tomorrow morning we'll have some honey for breakfast. Do Tiggers like honey?"

"They like everything," said Tigger cheerfully.

"So I went back to bed," said Pooh, "and Tigger slept on the floor."

"In the morning a tablecloth tried to bite me when I wasn't looking," said Tigger, "but I was too quick for it."

The Stranger ran his finger down the page until he found the proper place.

Pooh put the cloth back on the table, and he put a large honey-pot on the cloth, and they sat down to breakfast. And as soon as they sat down, Tigger took a large mouthful of honey . . . and he looked up at the ceiling with his head on one side, and made exploring noises with his tongue and considering noises, and what-have-we-got-*here* noises . . . and then he said in a very decided voice:

"Tiggers don't like honey."

"Oh!" said Pooh, and tried to make it sound Sad and Regretful. "I thought they liked everything."

"Everything except honey," said Tigger.

"So that's why getting honey is not a problem for me," said Tigger. "I don't like honey."

"So what can we learn about problems from Tigger?" asked The Stranger.

The room was very quiet while everyone thought about what their answer might be.

At first Pooh thought that the answer might be that he would have less of a problem getting honey if everyone was like Tigger because there would be more honey to go around and the only one to go around it would be Pooh. "Ummmmmmm," he thought. But he must have thought it out loud because Owl, who was perched next to him, turned his head and peered at him and asked him if lunch had not agreed with him because he was making a strange sound.

Pooh decided that his first thought was probably not what The Stranger wanted, even though it was a good thought.

Pooh liked honey, so getting it was a problem. Tigger didn't like it, so getting honey was not a problem for him.

"What . . . is . . . a . . . problem . . . for . . . one," Pooh said very slowly, "maynotbeaproblemforanother." He finished in a rush to get his Thought out before he forgot.

"Very good, Pooh!" The Stranger said excitedly. "That is exactly right, and everyone should remember that it is a very important aspect of the nature of problems. Deciding whether something is or is not a problem is a personal decision. While many things are considered to be a problem by almost all of us, it remains that the determination that something is a problem, or how serious it is, can vary from individual to individual. We say that problems are Steeped in Perceptions."

"Like the time we were trying to unbounce Tigger so we took him up to the top of the Forest, so he'd get lost and be less bouncy," Piglet piped up. "Pooh and Rabbit and I got lost in the mist, and we all thought being lost was a problem. Even Christopher Robin was anxious. But Tigger didn't think getting lost was a problem so he just went back to Kanga's, where he and Roo had dinner."

"I remember that," squeaked Roo, pleased that something he had done was being mentioned. "We played at fir cones too. But I forget how it ended."

"It ended like this," said Piglet.

And it was just as they were finishing dinner that Christopher Robin put his head in at the door.

"Where's Pooh?" he asked.

"Tigger dear, where's Pooh?" said Kanga. Tigger explained what had happened at the same time that Roo was explaining about his biscuit cough and Kanga was telling them not both to talk at once, so it was some time before Christopher Robin guessed that Pooh and Piglet and Rabbit were all lost in the mist at the top of the Forest.

"It's a funny thing about Tiggers," whispered Tigger to Roo, "how Tiggers *never* get lost."

"Why don't they, Tigger?"

"They just don't," explained Tigger. "That's how it is."

"So we can see from Pooh's problem with honey that individuals may vary in thinking that something is a problem," pointed out The Stranger, "and from Piglet's that everyone may think something is a problem but one individual may not. That's why we say that the determination that something is a problem is a subjective one.

"In addition, problems can often be insidious and may not even seem to be a problem at first," The Stranger continued. "They can come to you in a form that is difficult to recognize or disguised as something else."

"Like a gorse bush," said Pooh. "It looks like a harmless bush, but when you fall in it you get prickles in your nose and other parts, which is most unpleasant. Gorse bushes can be problems."

"Very much like that," agreed The Stranger. "In addition, sometimes problems have emotional associations that make them more difficult to solve. For example, if there is an element of fear associated with the problem . . ."

"Like trying to find your way home through the Forest and meeting a Heffalump with no one around to help, and you can't run because the snow is so deep and it's dark . . ." Piglet's voice was going higher and higher as he imagined a more and more fearsome situation. "And it is freezing and there might be two Heffalumps, one ahead of you and one close behind and they haven't eaten anything for days and . . ." Piglet ran out of breath and had to stop.

"It can make it difficult to concentrate on how you can find your way home," The Stranger finished for him.

Piglet shivered. "I would not want to have that problem. I'd wait until there were no Heffalumps around before I'd try to find the way home."

"That's called procrastination," said The Stranger.

"It means putting off doing something that you should do," said Owl, seeing the puzzled look on Pooh's face.

"Oh," said Pooh. "I thought he said 'poohcrastination.' Thank you, Owl."

"Many individuals do just that when they are faced with a problem," said The Stranger. "The problem with procrastination is that while you are avoiding facing up to the problem, it might get worse."

"A third Heffalump might come along," said Eeyore. "They often travel in threes, or so I've heard."

"Oooo!" said Piglet, sorry that he had thought up this example of a problem. He looked quickly around the room, just to make certain that there were no shadowy places where a Heffalump or three might be hiding, waiting to jump out at a passing Piglet. There were none, so he moved over closer to Pooh and settled down to listen to The Stranger.

"All emotions and all attitudes can have an effect on the process of Problem Solving and can have an influence on how satisfactory your solution may be. Often your emotions can make you think there is a problem when there really isn't. A good example of that was your adventure when Kanga and Baby Roo came to the forest."

"I remember that," said Rabbit.

"Me too! I remember too!" piped Roo.

"We thought that Kangas were Generally Regarded as One of the Fiercer Animals," said Pooh.

"They were different so we wanted them to leave the Forest," said Rabbit.

"But they were really very nice and now they are our friends so there wasn't a problem after all," said Piglet.

"Exactly," said The Stranger. "That is why we must always be very careful to be aware of the possible effect that attitudes and emotions may have on problems we are trying to solve. Sometimes individuals working on a problem will say something like, 'Let's get an unbiased opinion.' That means they want to be sure that emotions are not affecting the problem or the solution, so they get someone who hasn't been involved to review their work. Sometimes this is called getting a Fresh Perspective."

Pooh practiced saying "Fresh Perspective" under his breath several times, since he liked the sound of it. It sounded like the sort of thing that Owl might very well say. It ended up as "Fresh Poohspective," which was all right because he liked it just as well. Maybe even better.

"Is that all there is about the nature of problems?" asked Tigger, who had been restraining his bounciness for a long time.

"I'm afraid not, Tigger," answered The Stranger. "There is one more aspect of problems that I would like to talk about before we finish for the day."

Tigger bounced twice very quickly so that no one saw him. It relieved some of his bounciness, so he could listen as The Stranger continued.

"I wanted to mention that problems often don't come

one at a time. Frequently you are faced with several that you have to solve at the same time, or in a certain order. Can anyone think of one of your adventures where that was the case?"

"The adventure In Which Piglet Does a Very Grand Thing was like that," said Pooh.

"That's a good one, Pooh. Why don't you tell us about it."

"That was the day that it was very Blusterous," said Pooh, "and Piglet and I were going to Owl's house to have a Proper Tea with him."

The wind was against them now and Piglet's ears

streamed behind him

like banners

as he fought his way along, and it seemed hours before he got them into the shelter of the Hundred Acre

Wood and they stood up straight again, to listen, a little nervously, to the roaring of the gale among the tree-tops.

"Supposing a tree fell down, Pooh, when we were underneath it?"

"Supposing it didn't," said Pooh after careful thought.

"I think I remember," said The Stranger. "A tree did fall down, didn't it?"

"Yes," said Pooh. "But we weren't underneath it. We were in it."

"It was Owl's tree," said Piglet. "It was just as you said. There were a number of problems . . . all at one time."

"We couldn't go out by what used to be the front door," said Owl. "Something had fallen on it. Getting out was a problem."

"I was in a very uncomfortable position. Fallen downward under something with someone asking me to look at the ceiling, as I remember," said Pooh. "That was the first problem."

"And then there was how I was to get up to the letter box without falling and seriously damaging myself." Piglet shivered, just remembering.

"To say nothing of my no longer having a house," Owl said. "Being homeless is never easy and is almost always a problem."

"I know," said Eeyore gloomily. "From sad experience. But it *is* what one expects. Especially if it is cold and snowy out."

"That's a perfect example of what I was talking about," said The Stranger.

"How did they ever solve all those problems?" squeaked Roo, who always wanted to know how things turned out.

If Kanga had been there she would have said, "Now Roo, Dear, just wait. You'll find out in due time."

The Stranger said much the same thing only using different words. "If you don't mind, Roo, we'll find out later. Now while it's all fresh in our minds I'd like to summarize what we've learned about the nature of problems."

We have said that whether something is considered a problem is subjective, and the perception of its seriousness might vary from individual to individual. Problems can sometimes come to us disguised, or appearing to be something that they are not. The way we approach and solve a problem may be influenced by our own or other people's emotional factors or attitudes. Problems can be simple or complex. There may be more than one problem that we are faced with at a time, or we may have to solve problems in a certain order."

The Stranger stopped and looked around the room. "Does anyone have any questions?" He waited a moment. "If no one has, then I think we have covered enough for the day. I suggest we see what's in that second hamper."

What was there was enough for a Very Fine Tea, with enough left over for an evening meal.

While they were having their tea everyone told Roo how all the problems had been solved when Owl's house was blown down, and he fell asleep just as Pooh finished telling about the Very Grand Thing that Piglet did.

III

In which It Is Shown that SOLVE Is Not Just for Problems and Eeyore Endures a Moving Experience

Almost everyone was already there when The Stranger came by the next morning and arrived at Pooh's house. Small had gotten lost again and Rabbit was out looking for him, so they weren't there. Kanga had once more begged off as having to do housework she had been procrastinating about ("See," said Pooh to Piglet. "We were warned about that."), but she sent Roo along with Tigger. Alexander Beetle was still missing and some thought he might have buried himself head downward in a crack in the ground as he sometimes did.

"That's not altogether a bad thing," said Eeyore almost cheerfully. "Then one doesn't have to be careful all the time not to step or sit on him."

"Or Small," piped up Piglet. "Because he's not here too. Or is it 'here also' and 'sit on them'?"

"Or Small," Eeyore agreed. "Whatever."

Since it had been late the night before by the time the storytelling was over and Roo had fallen asleep, Pooh had ever so nicely offered to let The Stranger sleep on the floor of his house. But The Stranger told Pooh that he felt it would be an imposition, and he would stay at the inn in the village that was only about a mile down the road. Really just a pleasant stroll. He said he would see everyone in the morning, and they would talk about a different kind of problem.

After he had left, Piglet asked Pooh, "What's an 'imposition'?"

Pooh thought for a moment. "I think it has something to do with the way he curls up on the floor."

"Oh," said Piglet. "I just wondered."

When he came in, The Stranger apologized for being late and said that because of that he wanted to start right away.

"What I want to talk about," The Stranger began, "is that the SOLVE Method is not just for problems. Yesterday, we talked about problems and difficulties that you have had in your adventures. Finding breakfast for Tigger, getting lost in the mist at the top of the Forest, and Owl's house being blown down were all problems or difficulties you had experienced. The SOLVE Method will help with those problems. However, the SOLVE Method can *also* be a powerful way to improve situations or things that you choose."

The Stranger pointed to the tablet, which was still on

the easel against the wall. "You will remember that the first step of the SOLVE Method says 'Select the Problem or Situation.' Let me explain why the word 'Situation' is there."

"I wondered about that," said Eeyore. "I thought this was all about Problem Solving. I haven't heard anything about 'situation solving.' Adding on and confusing things just at the last minute is not helpful." He shook his head. "Not at all helpful."

"The reason we add 'Situation' to our Select step," explained The Stranger, "instead of just saying 'Select the Problem,' is that selection can be either a passive process or an active one.

"Passive choices are usually ones that are presented to you for solving, often by somebody else or by fate. A family member, a friend, your boss, your country or where you live, economic conditions, illness and so on, can all present you with problems that you need to solve. You were passive. The problem came to you. You didn't have to do anything to be put into the position of needing to solve it. A good example of a passive choice is the one we talked about, when the wind blew down Owl's house.

"On the other hand . . ."

"He means 'As distinguished from the first thing he was talking about,'" Pooh whispered to Piglet. Pooh had learned that from Owl, but he wasn't certain that Piglet knew.

"Thank you, Pooh," said Piglet. "I wasn't sure."

". . . active choices are the ones that you consciously make, usually in an effort to improve or make something better. The way you do it is, you decide to treat a situation as if it were a problem, even though it may not be one at the moment, and apply the SOLVE Method to it to improve it.

"As you get good at solving problems, you'll find yourself selecting situations for improvement more and more frequently. That's why we added 'Situation' to the Select step."

Eeyore shook his head at this. "I don't think I understand," he said. "It seems to me that there are enough problems to solve without going out and making things problems that aren't. Problems, that is."

The Stranger thought for a moment. "Let me give you an example and see if it makes things clearer. Let's use the time when Pooh and Piglet decided to help you. You remember, it went like this:"

"I've been thinking," said Pooh, "and what I've been thinking is this. I've been thinking about Eeyore."

"What about Eeyore?"

"Well, poor Eeyore has nowhere to live."

"Nor he has," said Piglet.

"You have a house, Piglet, and I have a house, and they are very good houses. And Christopher Robin has a house, and Owl and Kanga and Rabbit have houses, and even Rabbit's friends and relations have houses or somethings, but poor Eeyore has nothing. So what I've been thinking is: Let's build him a house."

"That," said Piglet, "is a Grand Idea. Where shall we build it?"

"We will build it here," said Pooh, "just by this wood out of the wind, because this is where I thought of it. And we will call this Pooh Corner. And we will build an Eeyore House with sticks at Pooh Corner for Eeyore."

"There was a heap of sticks on the other side of the wood," said Piglet. "I saw them. Lots and lots. All piled up."

"Thank you, Piglet," said Pooh. "What you have just said will be a Great Help to us, and because of it I could call this place Poohanpiglet Corner if Pooh Corner didn't sound better, which it does, being smaller and more like a corner. Come along."

So they got down off the gate and went around to the other side of the wood to fetch the sticks.

"I see what you mean," said Eeyore. "About making something a problem when it wasn't one in order to improve it. I had built myself a house and when I had left it in the morning, it was there. When I came back, it was gone. So that was a problem. It wasn't really gone. It had just been moved to the other side of the wood. I decided the wind had done it."

"But you said the house was better in places," said Pooh.

"And we said 'Much better,' " said Piglet.

"And that means it was improved," said The Stranger, who was a little embarrassed because he had forgotten that Eeyore had built himself a house that Pooh and Piglet didn't know about. So when Pooh and Piglet decided to build him one they used the house Eeyore had built to build the new one. Eeyore hadn't been told this and he still thought the wind had done it.

"I see," said Eeyore. "Pooh and Piglet made my house a problem even though it wasn't and it ended up improved."

"Yes," said Pooh and Piglet at the same time.

"In any event," The Stranger said, "things or situations that aren't problems can be improved by saying they are a problem and using SOLVE as if they were a problem."

Owl, who read the *Wall Street Journal*, looked wise and said, "I frequently see in the paper where companies are improving their costs in a particular area, or are developing an improved version of their product even though there was nothing wrong with the old one. So this would be a way to do that."

"Exactly," said The Stranger, "and individuals can use SOLVE to upgrade their skills or improve something about themselves or their situation that they find unsatisfactory."

"Like bounciness," said Piglet.

"I already bounce about as well as I can," said Tigger, "but maybe I could work out a way to go higher."

"Not what I meant," muttered Piglet, but Tigger didn't hear him.

"Kanga bounces higher than you do," Roo said help-fully. "Maybe she could give you lessons or you could use SOLVE to bounce even higher."

Piglet shuddered at the thought.

The Stranger said, "I think it might be almost time to have lunch. Let me review one more thing and then we'll see if the inn gave us good food in the picnic basket which I left outside so it would stay cool."

Everyone agreed that was a good idea.

"One thing that I want to stress. We decided that the nature of problems that came to you was that they could be simple or complex, single or multiple, subjective or come to you disguised, and that emotional factors or atti-tudes of yours or of those involved can affect your solutions and how you deal with problems.

"Now, the nature of the situations that you select your-self in order to improve them is exactly the same as the problems that are presented to you. The only difference between the two types of problems in the way you use SOLVE is in the S step, which we'll talk about after lunch."

"What I still don't understand," said Eeyore to Piglet while they were waiting for the picnic basket to be unpacked, "is how you and Pooh's deciding to build me a house ended up improving my house when the wind moved it."

"Probably we'll learn about that when The Stranger teaches us about the five steps of SOLVE," said Piglet carefully.

"The way things usually are," said Eeyore gloomily, "I probably still won't know even when we are all finished."

"I think that's possible," Piglet said. At least I hope so, he added to himself.

IV

In which the Select Step Is Discussed, Pooh Learns Right from Wrong, and Piglet Discovers His Name

"So far we have spent our time on the nature of problems," The Stranger began. "Now we will begin to talk about the way to solve problems.

"In order to use our SOLVE Method, we must have a problem for which we want to find a solution. That is the first step of our five-step method—to Select the Problem that we will work on.

"We must take care in this first step because, as we discussed, problems sometimes come to us disguised. Problems are like what Sir Winston Churchill—"

"Another Winnie!" said Pooh proudly.

"—like what Sir Winston Churchill said about Russia," continued The Stranger. "It is 'a riddle wrapped in a mystery inside an enigma.' We want to be sure we pick the *right* problem to work on."

Everyone looked at him blankly. Pooh didn't even say, "Oh, I see," which he usually said even when he didn't.

"Maybe a better way to stress that point," The Stranger said, "is to use the adventure when Kanga and Roo came to the Forest. They were new and everyone thought it was a bad thing because they were supposed to be one of the Fiercer Animals. It was decided that the problem was how to get them to leave the Forest."

As The Stranger was saying this, Roo was doing his best trying to look like one of the Fiercer Animals, but he didn't do very well, because Tigger thought he was trying to have a Funny Face Contest and made a face, making Roo begin to giggle. This, of course, ruined the effect because it is well known that the Fiercer Animals do not generally giggle.

"I remember," Piglet piped up. "The problem really was that we didn't know enough about Kanga and Roo to decide if they were a problem or not. All we knew was what they looked like, and I know *now* that sometimes mistakes are made based on appearance. It happened to me, because I was pretending to be Roo so we could kidnap Roo and scare Kanga into leaving the Forest. And Christopher Robin came by and didn't know I was me, because I looked different."

"I don't think I remember that," said The Stranger. "What happened?"

"It was just after Kanga gave me a cold water bath and strengthening medicine because I was supposed to be Roo and Christopher Robin came by. I tried to tell him that I was Piglet.

Christopher Robin shook his head again.

"Oh you're not Piglet," he said. "I know Piglet well, and he's *quite* a different colour."

Piglet began to say that this was because he had just had a bath, and then he thought that perhaps he wouldn't say that, and as he opened his mouth to say something else, Kanga slipped the medicine spoon in, and then patted him on the back and told him that it was really quite a nice taste when you got used to it.

"I knew it wasn't Piglet," said Kanga. "I wonder who it can be."

"Perhaps it's some relation of Pooh's," said Christopher Robin. "What about a nephew or an uncle or something?"

Kanga agreed that this was probably what it was, and said that they would have to call it by some name.

"I shall call it Pootel," said Christopher Robin. "Henry Pootel for short."

And just when it was decided, Henry Pootel wriggled out of Kanga's arms and jumped to the ground. To his great joy Christopher Robin had left the door open. Never had Henry Pootel Piglet run so fast as he ran then, and he didn't stop running until he had got quite close to his house. But when he was a hundred yards away he stopped running, and rolled the rest of the way home, so as to get his own nice comfortable colour again.

"And that was how I found out my full name," said Piglet. "Henry Pootel Piglet. That meant I had the same number of names as Edward Pooh Bear." Piglet paused. "As long as you don't count the 'Winnie-the-' part, that is."

"That certainly shows that mistakes can be made if you just go by appearance," said The Stranger. "When you are selecting a problem, you must be careful that you have selected the problem you want or need to solve. As Phaedrus wrote, 'Things are not always what they seem.'"

"Who is Phaedrus?" asked Owl, who liked to know about things like that.

"He was a Macedonian writer who lived almost two thousand years ago," said The Stranger, who also liked to know about things like that.

"That's a long time ago," said Piglet. "I wonder if things are always what they seem now."

Owl was blinking his eyes very rapidly because he was saying, "Phaedrus, Phaedrus, Phaedrus" to himself, so he would remember it in case he was ever asked.

"Now," The Stranger continued, "our first step in the five-step SOLVE Method is the S step. Who remembers what it stands for?"

"S stands for Select the Problem or Situation," said Piglet, looking at the tablet that was still on the easel.

The Stranger nodded approvingly. "Sometimes selecting the problem is easy and obvious, but, because of the nature of problems, we must always give some thought to making certain that we have selected the right problem."

"The way things usually are," said Eeyore gloomily, "I probably will pick the wrong problem. Why is that bad?"

"I think," said Pooh, "that if you don't pick the right problem, it's the wrong problem which means that you still have to solve the right problem after you've solved the wrong problem, if you do. Right?"

Everyone thought about what Pooh had said and after they had worked out the rights and the wrongs, decided that he was right.

"That's right, Pooh," said The Stranger, "but it's only half of the reason."

"So we need another half," squeaked Piglet. When he had gone to school in Christopher Robin's pocket once, he had been exposed to higher mathematics. Christopher Robin had taken him out of his pocket and he had seen written on the blackboard $\frac{1}{2} + \frac{1}{2} = 1$. After school Christopher Robin had explained it to him using a stick he had broken in the middle. Piglet was excited because now was his chance to make use of what he had learned.

"Yes," said Owl. "What is the remaining portion of the integer?"

"If we select the wrong problem," The Stranger explained, "as well as wasting our time and efforts, in some cases we may also limit our choice of possible solutions to the situation we find ourselves in."

"I don't understand," said Eeyore. "See, I told you I'd have trouble with this problem-solving thing. Maybe I should just give up." He shook his head. "Pathetic. That's what it is. Pathetic."

"No, Eeyore," said The Stranger. "Don't feel discouraged about having trouble. That only means that you may have to work harder, but in the end you'll learn it better. One of the world's greatest inventors, Charles F. Kettering, said, 'Don't bring me anything but trouble. Good news weakens me.' So don't worry, Eeyore, and *don't* give up. Another famous man, Thomas J. Watson, Sr., the founder of IBM, said, 'Success is on the far side of failure.' Now let me see if I can explain about how selecting the wrong problem can limit your chances for a satisfactory solution. In the case of Kanga and Roo, it was decided that they were strange and were Generally Regarded as Two of the Fiercer Animals, and the problem was that they were there in the Forest."

"Mostly it was Rabbit who decided," said Pooh.

"We decided also," said Piglet quickly, wanting to make sure that he got some of the credit if there was any.

"By deciding wrongly that the problem was that Kanga and Roo were in the Forest—" began The Stranger.

"Mostly it was Rabbit," Piglet interrupted quickly, "who decided, that is."

"—the only solution that comes to mind is to get them out of the Forest."

"Makes sense to me," said Eeyore.

"However, by picking the right problem—that you don't know enough about these new animals—all sorts of solutions are made possible. You can learn more about them. Find out if they really are Two of the Fiercer Animals. See if they could live only in a portion of the Forest. Set up a test period to let them stay and see if there are any problems. Learn if they might be good friends and on and on. There are probably a dozen or more solutions when you pick the right problem versus only one in this case if you pick the wrong problem."

"I see now," said Eeyore. "Thank you. That is much clearer."

"Good," said The Stranger. "At this point in our S step we want to decide and think about several things before we go on.

"The first is whether the problem selected you, or you selected the problem or situation. While you proceed with SOLVE in the same manner in both cases, if the problem selected you, you might want to review it to make certain you are working on the right problem.

"Second, evaluate if the problem is simple or complex and if it is a single problem or a multiple one. As we have discussed, if it is multiple, you will have to consider the order of working on the problems and their relative priorities, particularly in the O step.

"Thirdly, think and evaluate if the problem or situation has any emotional factors involved. Sometimes the problem or situation does and sometimes the individuals involved will have emotional associations either with the problem or with others who are involved."

"You mean . . . like if there is a Heffalump involved?" asked Piglet. "And someone who was afraid of Heffalumps was involved."

"Yes. That would be an example, but it doesn't necessarily have to be a negative emotion like fear or anger. You could have a case where the problem involved two other people and you liked one much better than the other.

That could affect the way you approach the problem and your solution."

"So what do you do," asked Owl, "if you find there are emotional factors involved?"

"Sometimes you can't do very much except be aware that they are there and very carefully examine your work to see that the emotional factors don't unduly influence you.

"As the final part of the S step, you should state the problem or situation as clearly and simply as you can. If you can't do this easily, it may be that either you don't understand the problem, or you may have selected the wrong problem. I often find it helpful to see if I can write what the problem is on one side of a single piece of paper. If you have difficulty at this point you should go back and rethink what the problem is, or clarify what you don't understand."

The Stranger paused and looked out the window, where it was beginning to get dark.

"Before we finish for the day I want to cover one more thing.

"You will remember that we said that SOLVE is not just for Problem Solving. It can be used for improving something that may not be a problem."

"Yes," said Eeyore. "I wondered about that. It seems to me it might be difficult to decide what should be improved since everything that isn't a problem right now might be improved. Which means there is more than one thing, maybe even three or four, that you need to decide about." Eeyore looked around the room. "I think."

"There are no specific rules, Eeyore," said The Stranger, "but you're right. It sometimes *is* difficult to pick out where to use SOLVE. It is mostly a matter of judgment, but there are some general guidelines. They are: Pick something that you think could be improved."

"Like a tail," said Eeyore.

"Yes," said The Stranger. "Or someone might want to look better, or lose a little weight."

"I did that once when I got stuck in the door of Rabbit's house," said Pooh. "I wouldn't want to do that again."

"Some people might want to save more money or improve the skills they use either at work or in their personal life," The Stranger continued.

"At work or on the job it's a little easier to decide what to improve. You select situations where there is lots of money or time involved, where safety is a factor, or to improve service to your customers or clients.

"In the end, it's mostly a matter of your judgment. If you do pick something to improve when something else might have been a better choice, you still will have improved something.

"Are there any questions on the S step of SOLVE?" he asked.

"No," said Pooh, after a minute or so of concentration. "I believe it is all straight in my Brain. I think I understand." The others agreed, except for Tigger, who was stalking a beetle who turned out to be Alexander, who had gotten trapped under the rug the last time he had visited Pooh's.

"Well, if that's the case," said The Stranger, "I think we have covered enough for today. Next time we shall learn to Observe, Organize, and Define Problems. Would meeting next Tuesday to talk about the O step of SOLVE be all right?"

"No problem," everyone said in chorus, except for Tigger, who had just bounced on Alexander before he recognized who he was.

V

IN WHICH Everyone Observes (the Second Step in the SOLVE Method), Tigger and Roo Are Stuck, and Pooh Hums a New Hum

"Hallo, Pooh!" said The Stranger.

"Happy Tuesday," said Pooh, hoping that it really was Tuesday but not being entirely sure.

"Happy Tuesday!" chimed Piglet and Eeyore and Tigger and Roo.

The Stranger set down the briefcase he had been carrying and looked at Pooh's friends thoughtfully.

"Well, well, well. I didn't know all of you were going to be here today or I would have brought along lunch."

Pooh worried, especially as he had eaten only a bit for his elevenses before gathering his friends together to meet with The Stranger. "You did say that we were going to meet and learn to Observe, Organize, and Define Problems."

"So I did, and so we shall. What did you think that meant?"

"Well," Pooh said, "when Christopher Robin was observing his birthday, it meant getting everyone together and having little cake things with pink sugar icing and singing songs. So when you said we would be observing, I made sure to ask everyone to come."

"But Kanga and Owl and Rabbit couldn't come," said Eeyore. "So they'll be the only dry ones once it starts to rain. Which it will do any moment now."

"I see," said The Stranger, chuckling. "Well, the type of observing I had in mind is not quite like that . . ."

Pooh began to worry even more about Needing a Little Something to keep up his strength.

". . . but perhaps we can have some fun anyway. I am glad you all could come along to listen. It's a bit cold this morning, so let's see if we can get a nice warm fire going. I think we can get started if you'll just help me."

"I can! I will!" squeaked Piglet, who began running back and forth looking for sticks and twigs for the fire while The Stranger collected some stones and rocks for a fire ring.

Pooh's worrying went away when the fire crackled to life and bright warmth spread out and enveloped him.

"This kind of observing seems a lot like the other so far," said Pooh, "except for the little cake things with pink sugar icing."

"At least until it starts pouring," said Eeyore, eyeing the dark clouds above.

"Tiggers like it when it rains," offered Tigger, looking up at the sky and bouncing expectantly.

"The type of observing I was going to explain today is the second step in solving problems," The Stranger said. "You remember yesterday we talked about selecting a problem and how some of them you choose and sometimes they choose you."

"Like when Tigger and Roo became stuck in the tallest Pine Tree," squeaked Piglet.

"That's right," said The Stranger. Piglet beamed, remembering how he and Pooh had been walking in the Forest. . . .

"Look, Pooh!" said Piglet suddenly. "There's something in one of the Pine Trees."

"So there is!" said Pooh, looking up wonderingly. "There's an Animal."

Piglet took Pooh's arm, in case Pooh was frightened.

"Is it One of the Fiercer Animals?" he said, looking the other way.

Pooh nodded.

"It's a Jagular," he said.

"What do Jagulars do?" asked Piglet, hoping that they wouldn't.

"They hide in the branches of trees, and drop on you as you go underneath," said Pooh. "Christopher Robin told me."

"Perhaps we better hadn't go underneath, Pooh. In case he dropped and hurt himself."

"They don't hurt themselves," said Pooh. "They're such very good droppers."

Piglet still felt that to be underneath a Very Good Dropper would be a Mistake, and he was just going to hurry back for something which he had forgotten when the Jagular called out to them.

"Help! Help!" it called.

"That's what Jagulars always do," said Pooh, much interested. "They call 'Help! Help!' and then when you look up, they drop on you."

"I'm looking *down*," cried Piglet loudly, so as the Jagular shouldn't do the wrong thing by accident.

Something very excited next to the Jagular heard him, and squeaked:

"Pooh and Piglet! Pooh and Piglet!"

All of a sudden Piglet felt that it was a much nicer day than he had thought it was. All warm and sunny—

"Pooh!" he cried. "I believe it's Tigger and Roo!"

"So it is," said Pooh. "I thought it was a Jagular and another Jagular."

"We can't get down, we can't get down!" cried Roo. . . .

"Are they stuck?" asked Piglet anxiously.

Pooh nodded.

"So the problem was that they were stuck in the Tree," said The Stranger.

"And that they weren't Jagulars," squeaked Piglet, "because they are Very Good Droppers and could have just dropped down if they were."

"And landed on you," added Eeyore. Piglet squirmed.

"Once we have decided what the problem is," said The Stranger, "in this case, that Tigger and Roo were stuck up in the Tree, the next step is to Observe the problem or situation, Organize the different parts, and begin to Define them.

"We do this by deciding where things are now, where we would like them to be—which would be our goal—and by noticing anything that might be in the way of achieving our goal." The Stranger paused for a moment to use a long stick to stir up the embers of the fire before continuing. "We've said that Tigger and Roo were stuck far up in the tallest Pine Tree. That is a good statement of where things were. Next we would look at where we would like them to be."

"On the ground," said Tigger, remembering what the Forest looked like from so high.

"So we could say that the goal was to get you and Roo back down onto the ground."

"But that's not all," said Pooh. "Not being Jagulars, dropping would be out of the question."

"That's exactly right, Pooh," said The Stranger. *That* kind of bear, thought Pooh. "And that is an example of something that is in the way."

"Like me," said Eeyore.

"No, Eeyore. Something that is in the way of solving the problem satisfactorily, which is called a constraint."

"Like Tigger's not being able to climb down backward," added Roo.

"That's right," said The Stranger. "So a constraint is something that keeps you from accomplishing your goal, or that complicates the solution of the problem."

"Bees are constraints," said Pooh, rubbing his nose and remembering how complicated it had been trying to get honey from the Bee Tree because of them.

"Yes," said The Stranger, "I can see that they might be a particularly painful sort of constraint for a bear. Constraints usually reduce or dictate the possible solutions or the options you have as to how you can solve your problem. For instance, when you were planning to capture Baby

Roo, one of the parts of your plan was that Kanga would have to be looking the other way. This is a good example of a constraint. It means that a plan in which Kanga was *not* looking the other way would not be an acceptable plan and would not work."

"And Kanga *did* look away," said Pooh proudly, "and our plan did work."

"Not completely, I don't think," said Piglet, remembering the taste of Roo's medicine and being a pig of a completely different color.

"So constraints are additional barriers or challenges that must be overcome to solve the problem," said The Stranger.

"And bees," said Pooh.

"And what happened next?" asked The Stranger.

Christopher Robin and Eeyore came strolling along together.

"I shouldn't be surprised if it hailed a good deal tomorrow," Eeyore was saying. "Blizzards and whatnot. Being fine today doesn't Mean Anything. It has no sig— what's that word? Well, it has none of that. It's just a small piece of weather."

"There's Pooh!" said Christopher Robin, who didn't much mind *what* it did tomorrow, as long as he was out in it. "Hallo, Pooh!"

"It's Christopher Robin!" said Piglet. "*He'll* know what to do."

They hurried up to him.

"Oh, Christopher Robin," began Pooh.

"And Eeyore," said Eeyore.

"Tigger and Roo are right up the Six Pine Trees, and they can't get down, and—"

"And I was just saying," put in Piglet, "that if only Christopher Robin—"

"*And* Eeyore—"

"If only you were here, then we could think of something to do."

Christopher Robin looked up at Tigger and Roo, and tried to think of something.

"Now it seems to me," said The Stranger, "that later on Eeyore does a Very Good Job of defining the problem and the constraints."

"Thank you," said Eeyore. "Probably just luck, that's what it must have been."

"No," said The Stranger. "It was well stated; you said—"

"*Getting Tigger down*," said Eeyore, "and *Not hurting anybody*. Keep those two ideas in your head, Piglet, and you'll be all right."

"And there you have it," said The Stranger. "*Getting Tigger down* is the goal . . ."

"And me too!" squealed Roo.

". . . and you too, Roo. And *Not hurting anybody*. A good example of a constraint, something that must be considered when you think of possible solutions. So we have created an accurate statement of what the problem was: Tigger and Roo are stuck up in a tree and we want to get them down without hurting anybody, and they can't climb down backward. The starting point is that Tigger and Roo are up in the tree, the desired goal is to get them down, and two constraints are that no one get hurt and that they can't climb down backward."

"Oh!" said Pooh suddenly, though he didn't quite know why. He was beginning to have a thought, but being a Bear of Very Little Brain, sometimes thoughts took quite a bit of waiting. Like playing his new game with sticks at the bridge. The time between when you dropped your sticks into the river and the time that you saw them come out under the bridge was the same kind of thing. So Pooh waited and waited for the idea, and kept saying "Oh!" over and over again.

"*Oh! O!*" Pooh exclaimed.

"What is it, Pooh?" asked Piglet.

"It's O. I just remembered when we were learning about management. There was an O in that too. It stood for organizing."

"So it did, Pooh," said The Stranger. "And that's a good way to remember this step too. Because we're doing much of the same thing here. We're taking a problem that we have selected—"

"Or that selected us," corrected Eeyore. "Forced itself upon us, that is. Even if we didn't want it."

"—and we're organizing it in a way that's easy to look at. We ask ourselves: Where are we now? and Where do we want to be? and also What else is important? Establishing the current situation, the goal we would like to achieve, and noticing any constraints, things in the way, as we examine the problem."

"So organizing is like getting ready!" said Piglet. "Like when you have invited Rabbit and his friends-and-relations over to tea, and you must run around and around getting everything that you need so that you'll be ready when they arrive, which is quite a lot as there are so many of them to get ready for."

"Why that's quite so, Piglet," said The Stranger. "Thank you for putting it so nicely."

"Did I say there were a lot of them?" added Piglet, just to make sure that he had let everyone know what it was like.

"Yes, you did. And when you organize a problem that you've selected—"

"Or that selected you," repeated Eeyore. "Forced, I'd call it."

"—it makes it easier," The Stranger continued, "to move to the next step—Learn, by Questioning All Parts of the Problem. But then, that is a subject for another day."

The Stranger stood up and began putting some additional wood onto the fire. Pooh moved back a little so that the sparks wouldn't singe his fur.

"Do you remember the rest of the story of how you were able to get Tigger down and not hurt anybody?" asked The Stranger. "The reason you were successful was that without realizing it, you were organizing the problem correctly and that made your solution a good one."

"Unless you were on the bottom," said Eeyore.

"What do you mean, Eeyore?" asked The Stranger.

And Eeyore recounted the rest of the tale—or tail, as he would have put it.

"I've got an idea!" cried Christopher Robin suddenly.

"Listen to this, Piglet," said Eeyore, "and then you'll know what we're trying to do."

"I'll take off my tunic and we'll each hold a corner, and then Roo and Tigger can jump into it, and it will be all soft and bouncy for them, and they won't hurt themselves."

"And that's where I said what the objective was," interrupted Eeyore.

"Yes," agreed The Stranger. "And then . . ."

When Roo understood what he had to do, he was wildly excited, and cried out: "Tigger, Tigger, we're going to jump! Look at me jumping, Tigger! Like flying, my jumping will be. Can Tiggers do it?" And he squeaked out: "I'm coming, Christopher Robin!" and he jumped—straight into the middle of the tunic. And he was going so fast that he bounced up again almost as high as where he was before—and went on bouncing and saying, "Oo!" for quite a long time—and then at last he stopped and said, "Oo, lovely!" And they put him on the ground.

"Come on, Tigger," he called out. "It's easy."

But Tigger was holding on to the branch and saying to himself: "It's all very well for Jumping Animals like Kangas, but it's quite different for Swimming Animals like Tiggers." And he thought of himself floating on his back down a river, or striking out from one island to another, and he felt that that was really the life for a Tigger.

"Come along," called Christopher Robin. "You'll be all right."

"Just wait a moment," said Tigger nervously. "Small piece of bark in my eye." And he moved slowly along his branch.

"Come on, it's easy!" squeaked Roo. And suddenly Tigger found how easy it was.

"Ow!" he shouted as the tree flew past him.

"Look out!" cried Christopher Robin to the others.

There was a crash, and a tearing noise, and a confused heap of everybody on the ground.

Christopher Robin and Pooh and Piglet picked themselves up first, and then they picked Tigger up, and underneath everybody else was Eeyore.

"Oh, Eeyore!" cried Christopher Robin. "Are you hurt?" And he felt him rather anxiously, and dusted him and helped him to stand up again.

Eeyore said nothing for a long time. And then he said: "Is Tigger there?"

Tigger was there, feeling Bouncy again already.

"Yes," said Christopher Robin. "Tigger's here."

"Well, just thank him for me," said Eeyore.

"I see," said The Stranger, laughing gently. "I hadn't remembered that part. I'm sorry, Eeyore. I hope you weren't hurt."

"It's all right," said Eeyore. "I only feel it when it's going to rain. Which should be any time now."

"There's one other thing I want to share with you," said The Stranger. "When we begin to work on a problem, this step is very important because how we Observe, Organize, and Define a problem often dictates how it is

solved. If we had observed the situation and had said the problem was not how to get Tigger and Roo down, but how to get Pooh and Piglet, and then Christopher Robin and Eeyore up into the Tallest Pine Tree, it would have been a completely different problem."

"A very Tall One," said Pooh.

"If we had said that the problem was to get Tigger and Roo down but left out the part about not hurting anybody—"

"That's the part I said," said Eeyore.

"—then the end of the adventure might have turned out quite differently," continued The Stranger. "So when we begin to solve problems, it is important to observe the problem carefully, to organize it by defining the starting point, the desired goal, and also to examine any constraints or difficulties that complicate the problem before taking another step."

"Especially if you are a Tigger Out On A Limb!" added Tigger.

"Well, I have enjoyed our talk and hope that you all had fun and learned about the second step in Problem Solving. Perhaps we can meet again if you'd like to learn about Learning."

The Stranger spent quite a few minutes using his long stick to move the burning embers apart and then spreading sand and dirt over them until the fire was completely out.

"That sounds twice as hard as just learning all by itself," said Pooh. "And learning by itself makes me hungry. Perhaps you could bring a Little Something to eat, just in case."

"That I shall," laughed The Stranger, who picked up his briefcase and walked off toward Owl's house, saying, "See you soon!" as he wandered out of sight.

Roo and Tigger bounded off together shouting, "Goodbye!" as they left for Kanga's house to play in the sand pit before supper.

"You did Very Well today, Piglet," said Pooh.

"Well, I *have* been to school, you know," said Piglet, making sure Pooh remembered.

"But now *I* have a problem!" said Pooh.

"That you're going to get soaked when it starts raining any minute now?" asked Eeyore.

"No, that it's too late for tea, but not quite time for supper. I know I won't be able to wait until supper, but then what do you call it if you have a little smackerel between?"

"That *is* a problem," said Piglet. "Well, you shall just have to come to my house. We'll think up a name for it while we have some. And you too, Eeyore."

"Thanks, no. I think I'll just stay here awhile and watch the rain. Perhaps I'll be struck by lightning."

So Pooh and Piglet wandered off toward Piglet's house, leaving Eeyore standing in the opening, eyeing the gathering clouds. As they left, Eeyore could hear Pooh trying out names of what you would call a smackerel that was too late for tea and too early for supper.

"Tupper! No . . . uh . . . let's see . . . How about PasTea? Or maybe . . ."

After a while Pooh decided that he would just call it "Snack," and in that way he could use the same name if he ran into the same problem with a smackerel that happened between breakfast and elevenses, or between lunch and tea, or whatever. He spent the rest of the walk happily humming a new hum, all about Problem Solving and what The Stranger had been teaching them, and it went like this:

> *Select the problem of the day,*
> *Finding one that's right to do,*
> *You can choose it either way,*
> *You pick it or it picks you.*
>
> *Observe it very carefully,*
> *"Where do I start? Where am I going?"*
> *And don't forget about the bee,*
> *"What's in the way of doing or knowing?"*

VI

IN WHICH Learning by Questioning Is
Talked About, a Horrible Heffalump
Is Trapped, and Pooh Finds He
Is a Very "Whys" Bear

"There he is!" Pooh and Piglet had spied The Stranger,
walking along the path that led to the open place where
they had met yesterday. "Hallo. Good Morning!"

"Good Morning, Pooh. Good Morning, Piglet. I'm
pleased to see you. Perhaps you'll walk with me the rest of
the way?"

They said they would, but didn't really, spending a
great deal of time hurrying ahead or dropping behind or
even wandering off to one side of the path or the other
when Something Interesting was noticed. After a short
while they reached the place and came upon Owl, perched
on a rock and looking around curiously. It wasn't that he
was being curious and looking around as much as it was
that when he looked around he was able to turn his head
completely in circles, and it was quite curious, unless you
too could turn your head that way.

"Hallo, Owl!" said Pooh.

"Hallo, Pooh," said Owl.

"Good Morning, Owl," said The Stranger. "Have you seen Tigger and Roo? And Eeyore? I thought they were going to join us this morning."

"They were here," replied Owl, "but they said something about going past Christopher Robin's house to play on the river where the Big Stones and Rox are."

"Well, perhaps they'll be back in a little bit, just in time for lunch," said The Stranger, lifting his picnic basket and placing it on a stump nearby.

Pooh looked longingly at the basket. "I hope they won't be too long."

"Let us get started anyway," said The Stranger, "and they can join in when they return. Now—"

"Why?" asked Pooh, really wanting to know how long they would have to wait.

"Because I think it would be better to get started, as we have a great deal to talk about," explained The Stranger.

"Why?" repeated Pooh.

"Well, because today we'll be talking about the third step in Problem Solving: Learn by Questioning. And there's a lot to it," said The Stranger.

"Why?" said Pooh and Piglet together, Piglet having caught on and wanting to be part of the conversation, as he was sure it was beginning to go Somewhere.

The Stranger looked back and forth between Pooh and

Piglet. "Because after we have Selected a Problem, or have had one selected for us, as I'm sure Eeyore would have pointed out if he were here; and after we have Observed, Organized, and Defined a problem by stating accurately what the problem is, where we're starting from, what our goal is, and if there is anything else we should consider; it is helpful to next find out as much as we can about it."

"Why?" This time Owl joined in with Pooh and Piglet.

"I can see you've gotten ahead of me," laughed The Stranger. Pooh looked over his shoulder thinking that if they had gotten ahead of The Stranger, then surely he would be behind them, but he saw only the heather and gorse bushes by the edge of the clearing.

"That's a Very Good Question," continued The Stranger. "One of the best, in fact. The reason why we ask questions during this part of the process is to confirm the facts of the problem or to verify some of what is already known. We might want to ask questions to find out things that we don't know or to fill in gaps in what we *do* know. We also ask questions to gauge the relative importance of different elements."

"What are 'elements'?" Pooh whispered to Piglet.

"I think those are a special kind of Heffalump," Piglet answered. "They are gray and have long tusks."

"Larger and fiercer than your normal Heffalump," added Owl, "and primarily found in wetter areas with greater precipitation."

"Why?" asked Pooh, again, proud of his determination to get to the Bottom of Things.

"Because the wetter conditions provide an increase in Floral and Faunal diversity which then engenders a greater environmental—"

"No. Why do we want to know those things?" said Pooh, having understood only the first couple of words that Owl had said anyway, and beginning to look around for Tigger and Roo and Eeyore, as all this talk was making him quite hungry.

"For different reasons," replied The Stranger. "Confirming facts or verifying what we already know is done to make sure that when we stated the problem, we stated it correctly. Finding out things we don't know, or filling in gaps in what we *do* know, helps us to understand the nature of the problem and what the problem is about. Finally, asking questions to gauge the relative importance of different ele . . . um . . . parts of the problem helps direct our attention to the parts that are most responsible for it being a problem in the first place."

"The problem parts!" squeaked Piglet.

"Just so," said The Stranger. "Piglet, perhaps you can tell us about the time you met a Heffalump? If I remember, that's a good example of just what we're talking about."

And so Piglet stood up, just as he had seen Christopher Robin do in school when reciting his work, and began his story. "Well, one day Pooh said . . ."

"Piglet, I have decided something."

"What have you decided, Pooh?"

"I have decided to catch a Heffalump."

Pooh nodded his head several times as he said this, and waited for Piglet to say "How?" or "Pooh, you couldn't!" or something helpful of that sort, but Piglet said nothing. The fact was Piglet was wishing that *he* had thought about it first.

"I shall do it," said Pooh, after waiting a little longer, "by means of a trap. And it must be a Cunning Trap, so you will have to help me, Piglet."

"Pooh," said Piglet, feeling quite happy again now, "I will." And then he said, "How shall we do it?" and Pooh said, "That's just it. How?" And then they sat down together to think it out.

Pooh's first idea was that they should dig a Very Deep Pit, and then the Heffalump would come along and fall into the Pit, and—

"Why?" said Piglet.

"Why what?" said Pooh.

"Why would he fall in?"

Pooh rubbed his nose with his paw, and said that the Heffalump might be walking along, humming a little song, and looking up at the sky, wondering if it would rain, so he wouldn't see the Very Deep Pit until he was half-way down, when it would be too late.

Piglet said that this was a very good Trap, but supposing it were raining already?

Pooh rubbed his nose again, and said that he hadn't thought of that. And then he brightened up, and said that, if it were raining already, the Heffalump would be looking at the sky wondering if it would *clear up*, and so he wouldn't see the Very Deep Pit until he was half-way down. . . . When it would be too late.

Piglet said that, now that this point had been explained, he thought it was a Cunning Trap.

"So you see," said The Stranger, "Piglet was doing a good job of asking questions." Piglet stopped squirming around where he was sitting and beamed proudly at the others. "When Pooh decided that he would catch a Heffalump, that was the selection of the problem to be solved. And Pooh's declaration that he would catch one by using a Cunning Trap was a result of his observations on the nature of Heffalumps, and his organization and definition of the problem of catching Heffalumps. Piglet's questions about why the Heffalump would fall in the trap and also about what might happen if it were raining already are also good questions that serve to help them examine the problem and fill in their understanding of Heffalumps and Cunning Traps."

"I learned that at school," squeaked Piglet.

"Did you now?" replied The Stranger. "Tell me about your schooling."

"Christopher Robin took me. He put me in his pocket," Piglet said, pausing to make sure that everyone was listening. "School was mostly about questions, as a matter of fact."

"Education often utilizes an interrogatory or Socratic forum for dispensation or transference of intellectual or pragmatic erudition," said Owl.

Pooh understood the words "education," as it was something he didn't have; "often," as it was how frequently he became hungry, like right now; and "or" and "of"; but the rest of what Owl said only served to confuzzle him. And he was much more easily confuzzled when he was hungry, he told himself. He looked around one more time, hoping that Tigger and Roo and Eeyore might just now be returning.

"Yes," Piglet agreed with Owl, although he hadn't really understood any more of what Owl had said than Pooh. "And if most of school was about questions, the rest of it was all filled up with answers."

The Stranger noticed Pooh's attention elsewhere, and guessed what it was that had him shifting and fidgeting and looking around. "Before we go on, I think we should have a bite to eat. I was going to wait for the others, but they'll be along shortly, no doubt, and there's plenty, so let's start without them."

Pooh was overjoyed and proved extremely helpful to The Stranger, unloading his basket and making sure exactly what everything was as he removed it from the hamper.

"One of the interesting things about questions," continued The Stranger as they all enjoyed their lunch, "is that sometimes the answers to questions require more questions to be asked."

"Like when you're having honey and condensed milk," said Pooh stickily, making sure that the honey that The Stranger had brought was really honey all the way to the bottom, and not honey-colored cheese of the kind his uncle had mentioned, "and it doesn't come out right and you have to have a little more milk to even out the honey and then a little more honey because now you've not got enough."

"Exactly," continued The Stranger. "Finding out all you can about a problem by asking questions helps you to understand all aspects of the problem and will be important when we talk about visualizing potential solutions. Now, let's see . . . how did the story continue?"

"I know, I know!" squealed Piglet, jumping up and down, finally settling down enough to continue. "It was right after I had said that it seemed a Cunning Trap."

Pooh was very proud when he heard this, and he felt that the Heffalump was as good as caught already, but there was just one other thing which had to be thought about, and it was this. *Where should they dig the Very Deep Pit?*

Piglet said that the best place would be somewhere where a Heffalump was, just before he fell into it, only about a foot farther on.

"But then he would see us digging it," said Pooh.

"Not if he was looking at the sky."

"He would Suspect," said Pooh, "if he happened to look down." He thought for a long time and then added sadly, "It isn't as easy as I thought. I suppose that's why Heffalumps hardly *ever* get caught."

"That must be it," said Piglet.

They sighed and got up; and when they had taken a few gorse prickles out of themselves they sat down again; and all the time Pooh was saying to himself, "If only I could *think* of something!" For he felt sure that a Very Clever Brain could catch a Heffalump if only he knew the right way to go about it.

"Suppose," he said to Piglet, "*you* wanted to catch *me*, how would you do it?"

"Well," said Piglet, "I should do it like this. I should make a Trap, and I should put a Jar of Honey in the Trap, and you would smell it, and you would go in after it, and—"

"And I would go in after it," said Pooh excitedly, "only very carefully so as not to hurt myself, and I would get to the Jar of Honey, and I should lick round the edges first of all, pretending that there wasn't any more, you know, and then I should walk away and think about it a little, and then I should come back and start licking in the middle of the jar, and then—"

"Yes, well never mind about that. There you would be, and there I should catch you. Now the first thing to think of is, What do Heffalumps like? I should think acorns, shouldn't you? We'll get a lot of—I say, wake up, Pooh!"

Pooh, who had gone into a happy dream, woke up with a start, thinking that Piglet was talking to him, and not just retelling part of the story.

"So you see," said The Stranger, "both Pooh and Piglet are asking questions to find out more about how they should go about trapping the Heffalump."

"How many questions are there?" asked Pooh.

"That is an impertinent question, Pooh," said Owl. "You should have been paying more attention."

"Now wait a moment, Owl," said The Stranger. "There are no bad questions. Or foolish ones, or even ones that are too simple or silly. This is Very Important. Any question must be regarded seriously no matter how basic or silly. Often, the simplest questions are the best ones because they address issues that are most fundamental or meaningful to a particular problem."

That kind of bear, thought Pooh.

"Let me give you an example," continued The Stranger. "Let us say you are a businessman."

"You are a businessman," repeated Pooh and Piglet. Owl stared at them.

"You might think it silly to ask yourself 'What business am I in?' as you would think that you already must know exactly what business it is you are in. You might say 'That's silly! I am in the book-publishing business' or 'I am in the insurance business' or whatever it was that you did. But if you question yourself and reflect more carefully on exactly what it is you do, and for whom, and how it is you really accomplish your work, you may find surprising answers.

"You may *think* you're in the book-publishing business, but really you are in the information-management business, which means you may be able to make other products as well: databases, audiotapes, multimedia CD-ROMs, or computer disks. Or if you're in insurance, you may realize that you're really in the business of helping people plan their finances, investing, and estate planning."

"If I were to plan an estate," added Piglet, "it would be quite grand, with lots of rooms and a large pool in the backyard."

"And a library and study," said Owl.

"And *two* larders!" said Pooh.

"So by asking questions," continued The Stranger, "even seemingly simple or basic ones, you can learn a great deal about whatever it is you are examining. The other thing about questions is that there are really only six different kinds. Do you know the five W's?"

"Of course," said Owl, "they were a world famous family of high-wire tightrope acrobats from many years ago. I think their name was Wallenda."

"Actually," said The Stranger, "I was thinking of the five 'W' questions: Why? What? Where? When? and Who?, which, along with How?, make up the six different kinds of questions."

"Who?" said Owl.

"Exactly," said The Stranger. "Using these six different kinds of questions on the different parts of our problem, we can easily generate a whole range of questions that, when we find the answers, will help us to understand the problem more fully."

"Who? What? When? Why? How? Where?" squeaked Piglet, trying out the six different kinds of questions and liking the way they sounded.

"You've got them all," said The Stranger, "but it is important that you use them in the right order too."

"There's an order to them?" asked Pooh, thinking that this must be Important, and trying his best to get ready to remember.

"Yes," said The Stranger, "the order is Very Important.

The first question you ask about any problem you are trying to solve is Why solve this problem? The reason that you ask this question first is that if you can't find a good reason, maybe you don't need to solve this problem at all!"

"That's the kind of problem I like," said Pooh.

"The next question to ask," continued The Stranger, "is What? as in, What exactly is the problem I'm trying to solve? In the last step, when we were to Observe, Organize, and Define the problem, we determined the current situation, the desired goal, and any constraints. Here, we ask ourselves What? to focus on the specific nature of the problem. If we are able to answer this question, it will help us to understand better and develop better solutions. But that's not all. For What? and all the following questions, when we find answers, we then also ask Why? and the Why? makes us examine the answers we get even more closely."

"So the precise order," said Owl, "is Why? and then: What? Why? Where? Why? When? Why? Who? Why? and How? Why?"

"Well done, Owl," said The Stranger.

Pooh felt he must have missed something. He could remember the five W's, and even the How, but now there were a lot of extra Whys all over the place, and it was making him hungry. "So . . . it's a good idea . . . to ask . . . Why? a lot?"

"Yes, indeed. When you ask Why? after answering the

other W questions, you are trying to find the reasons behind the answers and to understand the problem better. Here, let's use a quick example. Say . . . uh, er, suppose you were—"

"Hungry!" said Pooh.

"All right," said The Stranger. "The problem is that you are hungry. The first question we said you should ask is Why? as in Why should you solve this problem?"

"Why, because I'd much rather be full," said Pooh.

"The second question," continued The Stranger, "is What?, perhaps What are you hungry for?"

"Honey!" said Pooh, dreamily.

"And after we get an answer to one of our W questions, we then ask Why? Pooh, why are you hungry for honey?"

"Well," said Pooh slowly, "I . . . think . . . it's . . . um. I don't know why. Perhaps some cake would be nice too, or even some condensed milk."

"So we know now," said The Stranger, "that while you are hungry for honey, you could also be happy with cake or condensed milk. So we learned of two other ways to solve the problem that you are hungry."

Pooh's tummy began to rumble. "Does solving problems always make you so hungry?"

"Not always," said The Stranger. "So the order of the questions is meant to approach the problem's most important aspects first." The Stranger took a stick and wrote in the dirt so that all could see, and this is what he wrote:

WHY SHOULD THIS PROBLEM BE SOLVED?

WHAT IS THE PROBLEM?	WHY IS IT A PROBLEM?
WHERE DOES THE PROBLEM OCCUR?	WHY DOES IT OCCUR THERE?
WHEN DOES THE PROBLEM OCCUR?	WHY DOES IT OCCUR THEN?
WHO IS INVOLVED WITH THE PROBLEM?	WHY ARE THEY INVOLVED?
HOW DOES THE PROBLEM ARISE?	WHY DOES IT ARISE IN THAT WAY?

"But you still haven't explained why," said Piglet.

"Why what?" said The Stranger.

"Why *that* particular order?"

"You're right, Piglet," said The Stranger. "I'm sorry. The reason we use that particular order is that the questions are arranged to find out about things that are most easily or least expensively changed first. Changing *where* something is done is generally less of an undertaking, less difficult or costly, than changing *how* something is done. So if we can solve our problem based on an earlier question, it often is less troublesome or costly to correct."

"I always have trouble with the Hows," said Pooh.

"In our story," said The Stranger, "Pooh asks himself *Where* should he dig the Very Deep Pit and also asks Piglet *How* he would go about catching Pooh. Both are good examples of questions that will help them to solve their problem about catching Heffalumps."

"But not much help once you've got one," added Pooh.

"Well, let's see," said The Stranger, "what was the rest of the story?"

"Honey," said Piglet to himself in a thoughtful way, as if it were now settled. "*I'll* dig the pit, while *you* go and get the honey."

"Very well," said Pooh, and he stumped off.

As soon as he got home, he went to the larder; and he stood on a chair, and took down a very large jar of honey from the top shelf. It had HUNNY written on it,

but, just to make sure, he took off the paper cover and looked at it, and it *looked* just like honey. "But you never can tell," said Pooh. . . . So he put his tongue in, and took a large lick. "Yes," he said, "it is. No doubt about that. . . ." And he gave a deep sigh. "I *was* right. It *is* honey, right the way down."

Having made certain of this, he took the jar back to

Piglet, and Piglet looked up from the bottom of his Very Deep Pit, and said, "Got it?" and Pooh said, "Yes, but it isn't quite a full jar," and he threw it down to Piglet, and Piglet said, "No, it isn't! Is that all you've got left?" and Pooh said, "Yes."

"Well, good night, Pooh," said Piglet, when they had got to Pooh's house. "And we meet at six o'clock to-morrow morning by the Pine Trees, and see how many Heffalumps we've got in our Trap."

"Good night!"

By and by Piglet woke up. As soon as he woke he said to himself, "Oh!" Then he said bravely, "Yes," and then, still more bravely, "Quite so." But he didn't feel very brave, for the word which was really jiggeting about in his brain was "Heffalumps."

What was a Heffalump like?

Was it Fierce?

Did it come when you whistled? And *how* did it come?

Was it Fond of Pigs at all?

If it was Fond of Pigs, did it make any difference *what sort of Pig?*

Supposing it was Fierce with Pigs, would it make any difference *if the Pig had a grandfather called TRESPASS-ERS WILLIAM?*

He didn't know the answer to any of these questions . . . and he was going to see his first Heffalump in about an hour from now!

Of course Pooh would be with him, and it was much more Friendly with two. But suppose Heffalumps were Very Fierce with Pigs *and* Bears? Wouldn't it be better to pretend that he had a headache, and couldn't go up to the Six Pine Trees this morning? . . . What should he do?

And then he had a Clever Idea. He would go up very quietly to the Six Pine Trees now, peep very cautiously into the Trap, and see if there *was* a Heffalump there. And if there was, he would go back to bed, and if there wasn't, he wouldn't.

So off he went. At first he thought that there wouldn't be a Heffalump in the Trap, and then he thought that there would, and as he got nearer he was *sure* that there would, because he could hear it heffalumping about, . . . like anything.

"Oh, dear, oh, dear, oh, dear!" said Piglet to himself. And he wanted to run away. But somehow, having got so near, he felt that he must just see what a Heffalump was like. So he crept to the side of the Trap and looked in. . . .

"So we see," interrupted The Stranger, just when the story was getting interesting, "Piglet does a very fine job of making up questions about the Heffalump. And even devises a Clever Plan to find out the answers to them, being Very Brave at the same time."

"I think if I had gotten some of the answers," said Piglet, "I wouldn't have gone to the Very Deep Pit at all."

"And that's a good point too," said The Stranger. "Sometimes the answers to your questions about a problem may require that you go back a step and revise the statement of the problem or the goal or even add additional constraints. Often it can be helpful to go back and forth between the different steps of the Problem-Solving Method to make sure that your assumptions still hold. It's called iterating, meaning doing something over and over again."

Pooh hadn't quite been paying attention, except for the last part, when he thought The Stranger had said, "We should be eating . . . over and over again," which made quite a lot of sense to him just then. A Large Commotion began in the bushes to one side of the clearing, and out bounced Tigger, with Roo clutching tightly to his back.

"Whee!" squeaked Roo.

"Ow!" howled Tigger, stopping his bouncing just long enough to pick some prickles out of his fur.

"Good morning, Tigger! Good morning, Roo!" said The Stranger. "You're just in time for lunch. We've been learning about the third step in Problem Solving, Learning by Asking Questions."

"Like 'When would you like your honey, now or later?' and 'How would you like to pass the condensed milk, please?'" said Pooh.

"Well, not exactly like that," said The Stranger, "but I can see you're trying to solve your problem of being hungry, so let me help." He passed Pooh a jar of honey that he had brought along and began serving the rest of the lunch to the others. "Now, if you remember, Piglet had gone to the Heffalump Trap and looked in. . . ."

And all the time Winnie-the-Pooh had been trying to get the honey-jar off his head. The more he shook it, the more tightly it stuck. *"Bother!"* he said, inside the jar, and *"Oh, help!"* and, mostly *"Ow!"* And he tried bumping it against things, but as he couldn't see what he was bumping it against, it didn't help him; and he tried to climb out of the Trap, but as he could see nothing but jar, and not much of that, he couldn't find his way. So at last he lifted up his head, jar and all, and made a loud, roaring noise of Sadness and Despair . . . and it was at that moment that Piglet looked down.

"Help, help!" cried Piglet, "a Heffalump, a Horrible Heffa- lump!" and he scampered off as hard as he could, still crying out, "Help, help, a Herrible Hoffa- lump! Hoff, Hoff, a Hellible Hor- ralump! Holl, Holl a Hoffable Hellerump!" And he didn't stop crying and scampering until he got to Christopher Robin's house.

"Whatever's the matter, Piglet?" said Christopher Robin, who was just getting up.

"Heff," said Piglet, breathing so hard that he could hardly speak, "a Hell—a Heff—a Heffalump."

"Where?"

"Up there," said Piglet, waving his paw.

"What did it look like?"

"Like—like—It had the biggest head you ever saw, Christopher Robin. A great enormous thing, like—like nothing. A huge big—well, like a—I don't know—like an enormous big nothing. Like a jar."

"Well," said Christopher Robin, putting on his shoes, "I shall go and look at it. Come on."

Piglet wasn't afraid if he had Christopher Robin with him, so off they went. . . .

"I can hear it, can't you?" said Piglet anxiously, as they got near.

"I can hear *something*," said Christopher Robin. It was Pooh bumping his head against a tree-root he had found.

"There!" said Piglet. "Isn't it *awful?*" And he held on tight to Christopher Robin's hand.

Suddenly, Christopher Robin began to laugh . . . and he laughed . . . and he laughed . . . and he laughed.

"I think that I am getting a headache," said Piglet, remembering how foolish he had felt when the Horrible Heffalump turned out to be Pooh.

"Don't feel badly, Piglet," said The Stranger. "It must have been very easy to mistake Pooh for a Horrible Heffalump, especially since he was wearing a jar on his head and howling in the bottom of a Heffalump Trap."

"Although everyone knows," said Owl, "that Heffalumps are migratory and herbivorous and aren't usually found in this wood except in the spring."

Pooh didn't know this, and so tried to change the subject, saying, "Christopher Robin was Asking Important Questions in the story, wasn't he?"

"Yes," said The Stranger. "When Piglet presented him with the problem of having found a Heffalump . . ."

"Or what *looked* like a Heffalump," said Piglet.

". . . Christopher Robin immediately asked Where? and What? to find out more about it. So you see, asking questions is a very good way to find things out, confirm facts, and assess whatever problem you are facing. The six different kinds of questions will help you to do this: Why? What? Where? When? Who? and How? Remember too that the order of the questions is Important, and that when we find an answer to the questions, we then ask Why? so that we can try to understand the reasons behind the answers. When we've finished asking questions, we should know a great deal more than when we started, and we should begin to see ways we might solve the problem. And that will be our next step—Visualize Possible Solutions, Select One, and Refine It.

"Finally, remember: the questions you ask about the problem may give you answers that make you revise your statement of the problem, its goals, or the addition of constraints."

"Which are sometimes bees," stated Pooh.

"Oh, Bear!" said The Stranger fondly.

VII

In which Visualizing Possible Solutions Is Practiced, a Briefcase Is Rescued, and Pooh Adds Two Verses

Pooh and Piglet were walking in the Forest, when they came upon The Stranger standing at the edge of a Very Deep Pit with his hands on his hips and staring down at the bottom of it.

"Hallo!" said Pooh and Piglet at once.

"What are you doing?" asked Pooh.

"I am trying to Visualize Possible Solutions," said The Stranger.

"I don't see anything," said Pooh, looking down into the pit just to make sure.

"I mean I am trying to think of solutions to solve a small problem that I have," said The Stranger. "I was walking along this path, when I stumbled and fell, and it seems I have dropped my briefcase into this Very Deep Pit that someone has left here."

"A problem!" squealed Piglet. "Oh! Oh! A real problem."

Pooh quickly tried to think of the five steps in the Problem-Solving Method that The Stranger had told him about. He wanted very much to be Helpful. "Have you . . . uh . . . Observed the Problem?"

The Stranger stopped staring into the blackness at the bottom of the Pit and saw that Pooh was trying out the Problem Solving that he had been learning about. "Very good, Pooh. Why, yes, and let me tell you what I have learned so far and perhaps you can help me solve it now that you are here. As I said, I was walking along and tripped and fell, and my briefcase fell into the Pit. Once this problem selected me, as Eeyore no doubt would have put it, I Observed that I am at the top of the Pit, that I would like to have my briefcase back, and that there is a Very Large Drop from here to the bottom of the Pit that is keeping me from getting my briefcase easily."

"If you were a Jagular, it wouldn't be very hard at all," said Piglet. "Jagulars are very good droppers."

"So now we ask questions?" asked Pooh. Pooh tried to remember the correct order. "Why! Yes, that's it, Why?"

"Good," said The Stranger. "Because I would like to have my briefcase back, as I have lots of important things in there."

Pooh knew the next question should be a What? question.

"What . . . did you have in the briefcase?" asked Pooh.

"Pooh, I'm glad you remembered that the next thing to ask was a What? question, but I think we should rather ask, What is the nature of the problem? or What is keeping us from getting the briefcase?"

"What *is* keeping us from getting the briefcase?" said Pooh.

"Well," said The Stranger, "the Pit is Very Deep, and I cannot see the briefcase, and even if I could, I don't think I could reach to the bottom and get it."

Pooh was ready. "Why?" he asked.

"Why, because the Pit is so deep or my arms are so short, or perhaps both," said The Stranger.

Pooh thought of asking a Where? but he was sure the answer was Here! and he was about to ask a When? or a

Who? but was just as sure it was Now! and Us! so he thought hard and asked a How? "How exactly did you fall?"

"I was walking down this path," said The Stranger, "and I guess I was looking at the flowers there, when all of a sudden I tripped, and fell forward about here."

"And the briefcase was gone?" asked Piglet.

"Yes, quite," said The Stranger. "And then I got up and looked around and realized I had a problem. I began to go through the Problem-Solving Method, as we have done now, and was at just this point when you walked up. Which is good, in a way, as I did want to spend some time with you talking about the very next step in the process— Visualize Possible Solutions, Select One, and Refine It. So let's sit down and see if we can learn about this step and solve this problem at the same time. If we do, we will have two rewards—if we *do* solve it, of course."

"I still think it is important to know *What* is in the briefcase," said Pooh.

"If you think it will help," said The Stranger, "I had all of my notes for the book I am writing, my laptop computer, and some other papers and things."

Pooh was disappointed that The Stranger didn't have anything Good to Eat in his briefcase. "Are you sure that's all you had?" he asked, and The Stranger nodded.

"Now," said The Stranger, "we have reviewed the first three steps of our Problem-Solving Method. The next, Visualizing Possible Solutions, is the one I find the most fun. We'll see how creativity and experience are helpful in thinking up solutions, how you can take different approaches depending on the problem, and even some useful techniques that will help you come up with more solutions when you can't think of any. Of course, once we have thought of some solutions, we'll need to review them and pick the best one, and then spend a little more time refining our best solution to improve its chance of success."

"That sounds like a lot of work to do," said Pooh, ". . . before lunch."

"Then we should begin right away," said The Stranger. "And the place to begin is with creativity and experience. Both of these are very useful when it comes to solving problems. And, while some people might say that creativity is a thing that you either have or you don't have, I've found that it really is a way of being, of looking at things without judging them first, and that it can be learned and improved. And experience is just the remembering of having solved other problems in the past, and not forgetting the things that worked, and also the things that didn't. Let me explain. Do you remember that Blusterous Day when Owl's house came crashing down with both you and Owl inside?"

"Well!" said Owl. "This is a nice state of things!"

"What are we going to do, Pooh? Can you think of anything?" asked Piglet. . . .

Owl coughed in an unadmiring sort of way, and said that . . . they could now give their minds to the Problem of Escape.

"Because," said Owl, "we can't go out by what used to be the front door. Something's fallen on it."

"But how else *can* you go out?" asked Piglet anxiously.

"That is the Problem, Piglet, to which I am asking Pooh to give his mind."

Pooh sat on the floor which had once been a wall, and gazed up at the ceiling which had once been another wall, with a front door in it which had once been a front door, and tried to give his mind to it.

"Could you fly up to the letter-box with Piglet on your back?" he asked.

"No," said Piglet quickly. "He couldn't."

Owl explained about the Necessary Dorsal Muscles. He had explained this to Pooh and Christopher Robin once before, and had been waiting ever since for a chance to do it again, because it is a thing which you can easily explain twice before anybody knows what you are talking about.

"Because you see, Owl, if we could get Piglet into the letter-box, he might squeeze through the place where the letters come, and climb down the tree and run for help."

Piglet said hurriedly that he had been getting bigger lately, and couldn't *possibly*, much as he would like to, and Owl said that he had had his letter-box made bigger lately in case he got bigger letters, so perhaps Piglet *might*, and Piglet said, "But you said the Necessary you-know-whats *wouldn't*," and Owl said, "No, they *won't*, so it's no good thinking about it," and Piglet said, "Then we'd better think of something else," and began to at once.

But Pooh's mind had gone back to the day when he had saved Piglet from the flood, and everybody had admired him so much; and as that didn't often happen he thought he would like it to happen again. And suddenly, just as it had come before, an idea came to him.

"Owl," said Pooh, "I have thought of something."

"Astute and Helpful Bear," said Owl.

Pooh looked proud at being called a stout and helpful bear, and said modestly that he just happened to think of it. You tied a piece of string to Piglet, and you flew up to the letter-box with the other end in your beak, and you pushed it through the wire and brought it down to the floor, and you and Pooh pulled hard at this end,

Unibind®

Crawley   3 Oak Court | Betts Way | Crawley | West Sussex | RH10 9GG | Phone: 0845 130 5575 | Fax: 01293 529272

Edinburgh   Abbey House | 83 Princes Street | Edinburgh | EH2 2ER

info@unibindUK.com

www.unibindUK.com

and Piglet went slowly up at the other end. And there you were.

"And there Piglet is," said Owl. "If the string doesn't break."

"Supposing it does?" asked Piglet, wanting to know.

"Then we try another piece of string."

This was not very comforting to Piglet, because however many pieces of string they tried pulling up with, it would always be the same him coming down; but still, it did seem the only thing to do. So with one last look back in his mind at all the happy hours he had spent in the Forest *not* being pulled up to the ceiling by a piece of string, Piglet nodded bravely at Pooh and said that it was a Very Clever pup-pup-pup Clever pup-pup Plan.

"So you see, Pooh," said The Stranger, "you were being creative when you thought of having Owl fly up to the letter-box with Piglet on his back."

"But that's not what we ended up doing," Piglet pointed out.

"That's true," said The Stranger. "But part of the way creativity helps is that one idea reminds you of another, which lets you make up many possible solutions to your problem. From these, you can choose the best one. The more solutions you have to choose from, the greater your chance of success."

"But what about *this* problem?" said Piglet.

"We could send Piglet into the Pit and have him find the briefcase and throw it up to us," said Pooh.

"That's a terrible idea!" squeaked Piglet.

"Now, wait a moment, Piglet," said The Stranger. "One of the things about creativity is that it is very fragile, and nothing stops creativity more surely than saying an idea won't work or is bad."

"I just meant . . . uh, that . . ." stammered Piglet, "that the Pit is Very Deep, and I don't know how you would send me in, and even after you did, if I *were* to find the briefcase, I don't know if I could throw it up to you, and even after that I would still be in the Very Deep Pit and would feel a lot like the briefcase does now, I suppose, not knowing how or if it will get out."

"Those are all very good points," said The Stranger, "and when we select ideas later and begin to refine them, we shall take that into account, but while we are thinking of ideas it is important not to judge them ahead of time or pretty soon no one will have any."

"We should send Pooh into the Pit and have *him* find the briefcase and throw it up to us!" shouted Piglet.

"Yes!" said Pooh, thinking about how he could check to make sure that everything in the briefcase was all right before rescuing it, and that The Stranger might have forgotten about a little smackerel he had packed inside, and not thinking at all about how he might get out.

"So creativity helps us Visualize Possible Solutions by allowing us to think up many possible solutions to choose from, and it is important that we remember that no criticizing of ideas is allowed. Any idea serves by either being one of many, or by making you think of another idea that you wouldn't have thought of if you hadn't heard the first idea. Now, experience helps by letting you use other similar problems that you have heard about or have solved in the past. It can also help by giving you an appreciation of those solutions that work and those that don't based on your own or someone else's previous attempts to solve a similar problem."

"Just as in Owl's house, when Pooh was remembering how he had saved me from the flood," said Piglet.

"That's right," said The Stranger. "Pooh remembered solving a difficult problem in the past, and it gave him confidence to think of a solution when you were stuck in Owl's house."

"Or when Tigger and Roo were stuck up in a tree and I thought of a way to rescue them," said Piglet, as he reminded them exactly how it had been:

"I thought," said Piglet earnestly, "that if Eeyore stood at the bottom of the tree, and if Pooh stood on Eeyore's back, and if I stood on Pooh's shoulders—"

"And if Eeyore's back snapped suddenly, then we could all laugh. Ha ha! Amusing in a quiet way," said Eeyore, "but not really helpful."

"Well," said Piglet meekly, "*I* thought—"

"Would it break your back, Eeyore?" asked Pooh, very much surprised.

"That's what would be so interesting, Pooh. Not being quite sure till afterwards."

Pooh said "Oh!" and they all began to think again.

"But we didn't use that idea to rescue Tigger and Roo," said Piglet sadly, "though I really think it might have worked."

"But every idea is important," said The Stranger, "because it leads to the next idea even if it doesn't solve the problem itself."

"So what do we do for this problem?" asked Pooh.

"What do you think?" said The Stranger.

"Well," said Pooh, beginning to think very hard about the briefcase at the bottom of the Pit. "We could go and get Owl, and have him fly down into the Pit, find the briefcase, and pick it up and fly out with it."

"Very Good, Pooh!" said The Stranger.

"Do you really think it will work?" asked Pooh.

"Perhaps," said The Stranger, "but what is important is that we are generating more ideas, and remember, the more ideas we have to choose from, the better our chance of finding a successful one."

"Perhaps we should do what we did before," said Piglet.

"What do you mean?" asked The Stranger.

"String Theory," said Piglet, knowing once he said it that it sounded Familiar and Good.

"You mean Cosmic String Theory?" asked The Stranger.

"No, we'll call Owl and have him take a bit of string down into the Pit in his beak and put it around the handle and bring it back up to us, just as we did at Owl's house. Then we can pull the briefcase up from here."

"That's very good, Piglet," said The Stranger. "That's a very good use of your experience too." And Piglet felt very proud.

"But before we choose one solution," said The Stranger, "let's talk a little bit about how different approaches are useful for different problems. There are many different approaches you can use to come up with potential solutions to problems. A numerical approach, or using numbers, might be good for problems that deal with quantities of things. Graphical approaches can be useful for problems where drawings or pictures make solving the problem easier, like using maps to find your way. Analogy can be a powerful tool for developing solutions. This is where you compare the problem for which you need a solution with a similar process or event whose solution you know. That then suggests a possible solution for *your* problem. An intuitive approach to a problem would use your common sense to reason a solution for a particular problem."

"How do you know which one to use?" asked Pooh.

"Often, the problem itself tells you," said The Stranger.

"I don't hear anything," said Pooh, leaning over the edge of the Pit and listening carefully.

"Perhaps I should have said that your experience with other problems," said The Stranger, "and common sense should help you."

"But with all the problems there are," said Pooh, "common sense doesn't seem very *common.*"

"That's a good point," said The Stranger. "We'll help you to learn how to solve problems, so you can have uncommon common sense."

"I'd like that."

"But you can see that if your problem was finding your way, a numerical approach would be hard to apply and certainly wouldn't give you many possible solutions to choose from. That's another way to know whether you have the right approach—whether it offers good possible solutions or many of them."

"But what if you can't think of anything?" asked Piglet.

"In that case," said The Stranger, "there *are* some ways to generate more ideas and they're fun to do since they *are* a sort of game."

"Oh, oh!" said Piglet, jumping up and down and running around and almost falling in the Very Deep Pit. "Teach me! I want to play!"

"Actually, Piglet, I'm sure you already know," said The Stranger. "Remember before, when you said that if you were a Jagular you could jump right into the Pit because they are very good droppers?"

"Yes, but I was just pretending," said Piglet.

"Well, this part of Problem Solving is about pretending," said The Stranger. "What we do to create more ideas for possible solutions is to pretend that one part of the problem is different than it really is. Let me show you." And The Stranger took a stick, because his laptop computer was inside the briefcase at the bottom of the Pit, and wrote in the dirt:

Make it bigger
Make it smaller
Add something
Take something away
Exchange two parts
Remove something
Replace something with something else
Combine two elements
Free association

"The way we play this game is to take the problem we have," continued The Stranger, "and pretend that it is a little bit different. For instance, let's pretend that the briefcase is bigger. Much bigger. Bigger than a house!"

"But then you'd need a crane to get it out of the Pit!" said Pooh, imagining how big such a briefcase must be.

"Perfect!" shouted The Stranger. "That's exactly how to play! So one way to get the briefcase out would be to use a crane. Now since our briefcase is not really as large as a house, the crane *we* would need could be very much smaller. But without playing the game, we might not have thought of trying a crane at all."

"How exactly does that help us?" asked Pooh.

"What happens," said The Stranger, "is that when we change the problem in some way by making part of it larger or smaller, or doing any of the things we mentioned, it helps us to see the problem in a new light, to examine the relationship of the different parts of the problem to one another in a new way. And often that can lead to new ideas about how we might go about solving it."

"Let's keep playing," squeaked Piglet, and so they did. They imagined they were smaller, as small as Small, and could walk right down the side of the Pit. They imagined adding water to the Pit and floating the briefcase out. They imagined the briefcase with a jar of honey inside (this was Pooh's idea, as he thought it might help him to think). And they continued playing until they had tried all the different ways of creating new ideas and even a few that they made up themselves, which The Stranger said was perfectly all right and very much in keeping with the rules of which there weren't any (except the part about not being negative). The game really worked. In a very short period of time, they had so many ideas for how to get the briefcase that they had trouble keeping track, and The Stranger had to write them in the dirt so they wouldn't forget them.

"That was fun," said Piglet.

"But quite tiring," said Pooh, "and hungry-making."

"Then we should continue our Problem Solving to retrieve the briefcase," said The Stranger. "The next thing we shall do is to review the different ideas that we have had and choose one that seems the best, think about it more closely and see if we can improve on it, and then try it!" So they talked and talked about the different ideas. Pooh thought the crane idea was a good idea, although he had no idea where they might get a crane. Piglet wanted to fill the Pit with water and float the briefcase out, while The Stranger thought that the String Theory was interesting. In the end they used them all.

Piglet ran and found some string and brought it back to the Pit, where The Stranger was searching for a long stick of just the right type and another short stick that looked like a V.

Pooh walked around and around the Pit, staring down into the darkness and listening to anything the problem might want to say to him and where it might be, until he spotted the briefcase.

"Aha!" said Pooh. "There it is! Right where I thought it would be."

When put together, Pooh's crane idea, Piglet's filling the Pit with water idea, and the String Theory had reminded them all of fishing. Although there was some confuzzlement about whether and what kind of bait a briefcase might like, they set about creating their tool. Pooh broke twigs off the long stick The Stranger had found, Piglet tied one leg of the V-shaped stick to the string, while The Stranger tied the other end of the string to the tip of the long stick.

But try as they might, they didn't have any luck snagging the briefcase. The wooden twig hook would slide across the briefcase, but wouldn't catch it.

"Why isn't it working?" asked Piglet.

"Yes," agreed Pooh. "We've done everything just right and should be on our way to lunch, and yet, here we are, still up at the top of the Pit and the briefcase is still down at the bottom of the Pit and . . ."

"And what we can learn from this," said The Stranger, "is that even if you perform all of the different steps in the Problem-Solving Method exactly, sometimes it just doesn't work when you finally try your solution. Of course, that is a whole subject in itself, and one we shall talk about the next time we are together: the last step in Problem Solving—Employ the Solution and Monitor Results. We shall see that sometimes solutions need to be changed a little once they are put into use if they are to work well."

"But what do we do now?" said Piglet.

"Perhaps if we tied the string to Piglet," said Pooh, "and lowered him down into the Pit, he could attach the hook and then we could both pull the briefcase and Piglet back out again."

"Good idea, Pooh!" said The Stranger.

"Bu-bu-but what if the s-s-string should break?" said Piglet.

"And that's good too, Piglet," said The Stranger. "It's important to think of all the possible consequences of an idea. And it reminds me of when Eeyore joined in your game of Poohsticks. Do you remember?"

Now one day Pooh and Piglet and Rabbit and Roo were all playing Poohsticks together. They had dropped their sticks in when Rabbit said "Go!" and then they had hurried across to the other side of the bridge, and now they were all leaning over the edge, waiting to see whose stick would come out first. But it was a long time coming, because the river was very lazy that day, and hardly seemed to mind if it didn't ever get there at all. . . .

"I can see yours, Piglet," said Pooh suddenly.

"Mine's a sort of greyish one," said Piglet, not daring to lean too far over in case he fell in.

"Yes, that's what I can see. It's coming over on to my side." . . .

"It's coming!" said Pooh.

"Are you *sure* it's mine?" squeaked Piglet excitedly.

"Yes, because it's grey. A big grey one. Here it comes! A very—big—grey—Oh, no, it isn't, it's Eeyore."

And out floated Eeyore.

"Eeyore!" cried everybody.

Looking very calm, very dignified, with his legs in the air, came Eeyore from beneath the bridge. . . .

"I didn't know you were playing," said Roo.

"I'm not," said Eeyore.

"Eeyore, what *are* you doing there?" said Rabbit.

"I'll give you three guesses, Rabbit. Digging holes in the ground? Wrong. Leaping from branch to branch of a young oak-tree? Wrong. Waiting for somebody to help me out of the river? Right. Give Rabbit time, and he'll always get the answer."

"But, Eeyore," said Pooh in distress, "what can we —I mean, how shall we—do you think if we—"

"Yes," said Eeyore. "One of those would be just the thing. Thank you, Pooh."

. . . There was a moment's silence while everybody thought. "I've got a sort of idea," said Pooh at last, "but I don't suppose it's a very good one."

"I don't suppose it is either," said Eeyore.

"Go on, Pooh," said Rabbit. "Let's have it."

"Well, if we all threw stones and things into the river on *one* side of Eeyore, the stones would make waves, and the waves would wash him to the other side."

"That's a very good idea," said Rabbit, and Pooh looked happy again.

"Very," said Eeyore. "When I want to be washed, Pooh, I'll let you know."

"Supposing we hit him by mistake?" said Piglet anxiously.

"Or supposing you missed him by mistake," said Eeyore. "Think of all the possibilities, Piglet, before you settle down to enjoy yourselves."

"And that is the point, Piglet," said The Stranger. "We should think of all the possibilities before we try something."

So they tried tying Piglet to the string and tried lifting him up only a short distance in the air and setting him down again to see if the string would hold, and it did. Then they had Piglet pick up a large stone that The Stranger said would be about the weight of the briefcase, and the string still held, although Piglet was still feeling uneasy about being let down into the Pit. He wasn't quite sure that Pooh had checked completely to see if any Heffalumps might have been trapped there recently.

But Piglet remained brave and Pooh and The Stranger lowered him gently down to the bottom of the Pit, and Piglet attached the hook to the briefcase, stepped on top, and was lifted right out and set gently on the ground.

"Hooray!" they cried.

"We SOLVE'd it! We SOLVE'd it!" cried Piglet, untying himself and running around in circles.

They congratulated one another and walked on to a small clearing next to the river where they sat on some rocks, and The Stranger checked inside the briefcase to make sure nothing had fallen out when it fell into the Pit.

Pooh watched over The Stranger's shoulder, hoping

that there was a forgotten treat inside, but there wasn't.

"So what we have learned today," started The Stranger, "is how to Visualize Possible Solutions, the fourth step in the Problem-Solving Method. We saw how creativity and experience are helpful when trying to think of possible solutions for your problems, and how we use different approaches depending on the type of problem we are trying to solve."

"The Game! We played the Game!" said Piglet.

"That's right," said The Stranger. "We played a Game to help us think of more ideas for ways to solve our problem." Taking out his laptop computer, he showed Pooh and Piglet the different ways that can be used to pretend to change things about a problem:

"We talked about reviewing and selecting problems," continued The Stranger, "and we discussed refining the solution that we chose to make our chance of success even better. And even though we didn't talk about the last step in the Problem-Solving Method—Employ the Solution and Monitor Results—we did get a chance to try out everything that we talked about in rescuing my briefcase from the Very Deep Pit. Thank you both for all your help."

Pooh and Piglet both felt very proud.

The Stranger said good-bye and that he would meet them again on Tuesday, by the Six Tall Trees, if they would like to have lunch with him and learn about Employing and Monitoring Solutions, and then he left.

Pooh and Piglet, after playing a few games of Pooh-sticks, of which Pooh won twenty-three to Piglet's nineteen, walked to Piglet's house. After the briefest of snacks, as he only wanted just a smackerel to hold him over until he got home, and as the Poohsticks games had been so close and all the excitement had hungered him, Pooh left Piglet's house and began to walk home. And as he walked, he began to hum his Problem-Solving Tune, and even added two new verses. It went something like this:

Select the problem of the day,
Finding one that's right to do,
You can choose it either way,
You pick it or it picks you.

Observe it very carefully,
"Where do I start? Where am I going?"
And don't forget about the bee,
"What's in the way of doing or knowing?"

Learn all you can by asking a lot,
But in the right order, as they are now,
Mostly Whys and then some Whats,
Then Where and When and Who and How.

(And after each, ask Why again.)

Vis-u-a-lize ideas, of course,
We think our thoughts and hope that they
Will put the cart behind the horse,
And not around the other way.

VIII

In which Employ (the Last and Most Important Step in the SOLVE Method) Is Tied Down and Some Other Things Float Away

"Oh, no!" cried Piglet.

"Oh, no!" cried Pooh.

They watched as The Stranger's picnic basket drifted lazily away from the riverbank.

"Pooh, you pushed the basket into the river!" squeaked Piglet.

"I did not! It fell," said Pooh. "I was just checking it, and it fell."

"Quick, Pooh," said The Stranger, "what is the problem?"

"The problem is that I see lunch moving downstream and sinking lower and lower!"

"Now, Pooh," said The Stranger, "this is your chance to do some really creative Problem Solving, not to mention rescuing our lunch from the river, and us from a hungry walk back. Quick! What do we do first?"

Pooh stared longingly at the hamper as it turned slightly and began to float a little more quickly with the current. "Bother! This problem has selected us! I went to peek inside, not to take anything, mind you, but just to see that there was enough for later . . . and that it was well wrapped up. It must have been perched Very Precariously, or it wouldn't have gone off and fallen into the river."

Pooh continued to follow the progress of the basket, and Piglet did too, as he was walking along the riverbank to keep up with it. "Observing . . . the problem is that my hunger is here in my tummy while my lunch is floating out there. And my goal is to have the lunch and my tummy in the same place, at least for as long as it may take to eat it. And the constraints in this case are *not* bees, but the river, which is wet and wide and not very friendly to bears who cannot swim!"

"Well done, Pooh!" said The Stranger. "That's very good work so far. What shall we do next?"

Pooh wondered for a moment why The Stranger didn't seem upset by the fact that *his* lunch was slowly drifting downstream, but as he was a Bear of Very Little Brain, and since it took all of his concentration to keep up with Piglet without crashing into gorse bushes, he didn't wonder for long.

"Uh . . . next we must ask questions," said Pooh.

"There it is! There it goes!" squealed Piglet, having crawled up onto a rock next to the river to get a better view.

"Why. Why solve this problem?" said Pooh to himself. "Why that's clear, because it's lunchtime. Then we ask What? What is the problem? Well, it is clear that we must rescue the lunch basket from the river before it drifts away and before it sinks. Let's see . . . then we ask Where? Piglet? Where is it going, Piglet?"

"Down, Pooh."

"Yes, but down *where?*" asked Pooh.

"Down the river. I expect it's going to the same place that the river goes, although you can never tell," said Piglet.

"And where does the river go from here?" asked The Stranger.

"It goes out past Kanga's house and the Sand Pit, under the bridge where we play Poohsticks, and on through the Forest," said Piglet.

Pooh wished that the basket *was* a Poohstick, so that they could wait for it at the bridge and then capture it as it went past. "Piglet, when will the basket arrive at the bridge and who will be waiting for it when it does?"

Piglet stopped chasing the progress of the basket long enough to realize that Pooh had a Plan. "Soon, and we will, won't we, Pooh?"

"Yes we will," said Pooh. "Now all we have to figure is the How. Oh, I'm always coming up against Hows."

"What is it, Pooh?" asked The Stranger.

"Well," said Pooh, "I have decided that the basket is following the river and will probably continue to, although you can never be sure, and that it will pass underneath the bridge very soon, where we shall be waiting to rescue it."

"Well done, Pooh," said The Stranger. "And how will you do that?"

"I haven't quite worked it out yet. Perhaps by hooshing, as we did with Eeyore, when he was a Poohstick. Or perhaps the way we rescued your briefcase from the Heffalump trap, by fishing for it, although we haven't any string and I don't think it will wait for us while I send Piglet home to get some. As you see, I'm not quite sure."

"But you are having a great many good ideas," said The Stranger.

"A stick! That's it! A Poohstick!" shouted Piglet.

"What about a Poohstick?" asked Pooh.

"We can use a Poohstick," said Piglet. "A little Bigger and Heavier, but a Poohstick just the same. Will you help us?" Piglet asked, looking at The Stranger.

"Of course," said The Stranger. "What is it you want me to do?"

"I thought," said Piglet, trying to explain and keep an eye on the basket as they walked along, "that we could use Pooh's Plan, and go to the bridge, and you could use a stick to fish the basket out of the river while Pooh and I held onto your legs to keep you from falling in."

"Splendid, Piglet!" said Pooh.

"So now we have a Plan," said The Stranger. "And it sounds like a Very Clever Plan, indeed. And this reminds me of the time of the flood. Do you remember?"

"How could I forget!" said Piglet, and he shivered.

"Yes," said The Stranger, "and your adventures then and our problem now are just the thing I was going to talk to you about today before my basket fell into the river."

"It was pushed!" said Piglet.

"It fell!" said Pooh.

"No matter," continued The Stranger. "What I was going to tell you about was the last and most important step in the Problem-Solving Method: Employ the Solution and Monitor Results."

"Why is it the most important step?" asked Piglet.

"Because," said The Stranger, "of all that has gone before. We have done a great deal of work to get to the last step, and all of our efforts will be wasted if we don't Employ our Solution."

"So what do we have to do?" asked Pooh.

"Once you have Selected," continued The Stranger, "Observed and Learned all about your problem, and you have Visualized Possible Solutions and chosen one, the final step is to put that solution into place. The way that is done is to 'create a path from here to there,' then 'test on a small scale,' and finally to 'Employ Your Solution and Monitor Results.' "

"Creating paths and testing scales," said Pooh. "That sounds like it could take a long time. I fear the basket won't slow down long enough to let you finish doing all that before it goes past the bridge."

"No, no, no," said The Stranger. "This won't take long,

and we can talk as we go. When we are ready to Employ
the Solution we've come up with, the first thing we do is
to 'create a path from here to there.' That is another way
of saying that we develop an action plan. An Action Plan
is a summary of all the things that we need to do or to
assemble to be ready to implement our plan. Remember
when Piglet was stuck inside his house by the flood?"

So as they walked alongside the river, with Piglet
scrambling up and down among the rocks and bushes next
to the edge, the better to keep sight of the basket, lazily
drifting with the current, The Stranger told the story again
of how it had rained for days and days, how the water had
risen in the Forest, and how Piglet had found himself surrounded by water and trapped in his home.

"It's a little Anxious," he said to himself, "to be a
Very Small Animal Entirely Surrounded by Water.
Christopher Robin and Pooh could escape by Climbing
Trees, and Kanga could escape by Jumping, and Rabbit
could escape by Burrowing, and Owl could escape by
Flying, and Eeyore could escape by—by Making a Loud
Noise Until Rescued, and here am I, surrounded by wa-
ter and I can't do *anything*."

It went on raining, and every day the water got a
little higher, until now it was nearly up to Piglet's window . . . and still he hadn't done anything.

"There's Pooh," he thought to himself. "Pooh hasn't
much brain, but he never comes to any harm. He does
silly things and they turn out right. There's Owl. Owl

hasn't exactly got Brain, but he Knows Things. He would know the Right Thing to Do when Surrounded by Water. There's Rabbit. He hasn't Learnt in Books, but he can always Think of a Clever Plan. There's Kanga. She isn't Clever, Kanga isn't, but she would be so anxious about Roo that she would do a Good Thing to Do without thinking about it. And then there's Ee-yore. And Eeyore is so miserable anyhow that he wouldn't mind about this. But I wonder what Christopher Robin would do?"

Then suddenly he remembered a story which Christopher Robin had told him about a man on a desert island who had written something in a bottle and thrown it in the sea; and Piglet thought that if he wrote something in a bottle and threw it in the water, perhaps somebody would come and rescue *him!*

He left the window and began to search his house, all of it that wasn't under water, and at last he found a pencil and a small piece of dry paper, and a bottle with a cork to it. And he wrote on one side of the paper:

HELP!

PIGLET (ME)

and on the other side:

IT'S ME PIGLET, HELP HELP.

Then he put the paper in the bottle, and he corked the bottle up as tightly as he could, and he leant out of

his window as far as he could lean without falling in, and he threw the bottle as far as he could throw—*splash!*—and in a little while it bobbed up again on the water; and he watched it floating slowly away in the distance, until his eyes ached with looking, and sometimes he thought it was the bottle, and sometimes he thought it was just a ripple on the water which he was following, and then suddenly he knew that he would never see it again and that he had done all that he could do to save himself.

When The Stranger had finished, he and Pooh walked along in silence for a moment or two. They could see the bridge up ahead around a bend in the river and with the sight of it Pooh's heart leaped, or perhaps it was his tummy, at the prospect of being close to the successful conclusion of this adventure. So he hoped.

"So you can see that Piglet does an excellent job of using someone else's solution, in this case a story that Christopher Robin had told him, to solve his own problem." At this Piglet stopped his scrambling along the riverside for a moment and smiled proudly. "But more important for us, we see that once he had settled on his plan, using a note in a bottle to call for help, he necessarily had to have a note, for which he would need a pencil, and a piece of paper, and a bottle in which to place it."

"And a cork!" added Piglet.

"That's right," said The Stranger, "and a cork to keep

the note dry and to allow the bottle to float. Having assembled his paper, pencil, bottle—"

"And cork!" said Piglet.

"—and cork," continued The Stranger, "he had to sit down and write the note, place the note inside the bottle, cork it tightly, and then throw it as far as he could out of his window. Each one of those things was an Action taken by Piglet to put his plan to work. Hence the term Action Plan, which is another way of saying 'creating a path from here to there.'"

Pooh thought about what The Stranger had said, but mostly he thought about the word "Hence," for he liked the sound of it, and it seemed to be the kind of word that Owl might use.

"So when we have chosen a solution," continued The Stranger, "we create an Action Plan that lists all of the things we must get or do to be able to put our plan into use. Now you have said that to rescue our basket, you want me to use a stick and lean over the bridge while you hold me, and I am to snag the basket. What is our Action Plan?"

"We must get to the bridge first!" said Piglet, hurrying now.

"And we must find a stick," said Pooh. "And it must be a Special Poohstick. One that is Bigger and Longer than most."

The Stranger hurried to keep up, and Pooh and Piglet raced ahead, with Piglet running up onto the bridge and turning to look back upstream for the basket. Pooh had turned off before reaching the bridge and was searching around on the ground for just the right stick as The Stranger arrived.

"I see it! I see it!" cried Piglet.

The Stranger leaned forward over the railing to look as Pooh came up with a stick that would be no good at all for Poohsticks, but which he thought would be right for fishing baskets out of rivers.

The basket was still upstream. "Here, Pooh," The Stranger said, "give me the stick and I shall tell you about the next part of Employing the Solution, while I practice. That is called 'testing on a small scale.'" And with this, The Stranger took the stick and got down on the bridge, leaning through the railings while holding the stick in one hand.

"But what are you doing? The basket isn't here yet," said Piglet.

"Now that we have done everything our Action Plan called for," said The Stranger, "it is often useful, especially with large or complex problems, to try them out in a very small way to see if they work before committing yourself to them completely. That way, if the solution doesn't work exactly as you had thought, you have the chance to alter or modify it before using it in a big way. Like this."

The Stranger asked Pooh and Piglet to hold tight to his legs as he stretched out and began to swing the stick back and forth. He was able to touch the end of the stick into the river, and splashed back and forth once or twice to get the feel of it. And then he tried to pretend that he was snagging a basket just to see how it might go. After a minute, he got up.

"There," he said, "that was quite good. I was testing our solution to see how it might work, and I think it might work just fine."

Pooh was very happy, as it meant that he might soon have something to eat, which he needed quite badly now, what with all the excitement and Problem Solving that he had been doing. The Stranger continued to explain.

"When we begin to Employ a Solution, we want to test on a small scale. The reason we do this is that it allows us to conserve resources and make sure our solution is a good one before we fully commit to it. We will use the same method when we are testing on a small scale as when we are employing a full-scale solution. We need to remember what our goal was so that we can be sure just exactly how we define success, and we need to select criteria that we will use to measure the results of our solution."

· "What's a criteria?" asked Piglet.

"That's a place where you stand in line and pick out all your favorite foods," said Pooh, remembering what Christopher Robin had told him about it.

"No, Pooh," said The Stranger, "that's something else altogether. Criteria are standards we can use to judge whether or not our solution was successful. Like a yardstick."

Pooh knew all about yardsticks, but only so far as they made excellent pirate swords and were also useful for pushing your paper boats away from the sides of streams where they had gotten stuck on twigs and roots and such.

"For this problem," continued The Stranger, "we could use as criteria whether or not we snag the basket, whether or not the contents have gotten wet, or if they have, how much of them. Those are all things we can check after we Employ our Solution to see just how successful we have been."

"What if we aren't able to snag the basket?" asked Piglet.

"We shall all starve," said Pooh seriously.

"That's a good point, Piglet," said The Stranger. "When we are beginning to Employ our Solution, it is a good idea to have a fallback option in mind. If things do not go very well, we have an alternative that we've thought of beforehand. To be prepared."

"So if we miss the basket," said Piglet, "a fallback option would be that we go farther downstream and begin hooshing the basket."

"Yes," said The Stranger. "But let's hope our solution doesn't require that. How soon till it arrives, Piglet?"

"It's moving rather slowly," said Piglet, "but I would think another minute or two before it arrives."

"Well then," said The Stranger, "I just have time to remember a little more of the story about the flood and your rescue of Piglet."

And so The Stranger continued the story:

> And it was on the morning of the fourth day that Piglet's bottle came floating past him, and with one loud cry of "Honey!" Pooh plunged into the water, seized the bottle, and struggled back to his tree again.
>
> "Bother!" said Pooh, as he opened it. "All that wet for nothing. What's that bit of paper doing?"
>
> He took it out and looked at it.
>
> "It's a Missage," he said to himself, "that's what it is. And that letter is a 'P,' and so is that, and so is that, and 'P' means 'Pooh,' so it's a very important Missage to me, and I can't read it. I must find Christopher Robin or Owl or Piglet, one of those Clever Readers who can read things, and they will tell me what this missage means. Only I can't swim. Bother!"
>
> Then he had an idea, and I think that for a Bear of Very Little Brain, it was a good idea. He said to himself:
>
> "If a bottle can float, then a jar can float, and if a

jar floats, I can sit on the top of it, if it's a very big jar."

So he took his biggest jar, and corked it up. "All boats have to have a name," he said, "so I shall call mine The Floating Bear." And with these words he dropped his boat into the water and jumped in after it.

For a little while Pooh and *The Floating Bear* were uncertain as to which of them was meant to be on the top, but after trying one or two different positions, they settled down with *The Floating Bear* underneath and Pooh triumphantly astride it, paddling vigorously with his feet.

"If I had *The Floating Bear* here," said Pooh, "I would be able to go and rescue the basket straight away!"

"But the part of this story that I wanted to share," said the Stranger, "was the part where, after you had chosen your solution, *The Floating Bear*, you still had to change your position several times before you got the hang of it. And that changing, once you've Employed a Solution, is very useful to Problem Solving. One mustn't be so attached to a particular solution that it isn't changed for the better as you go along."

"Here it comes!" squeaked Piglet. "Get ready!"

"One more thing," said The Stranger. "When we Employ the Solution we've chosen, it is important to really watch for signs as to whether the solution is working or not. When we see or hear that our solution is not working, or not working as well as we would like, we can still change and adapt it, whereas if we aren't open to the signs, our solution could fail and we wouldn't have a clue as to why. This is called 'feedback,' and—"

"Feedback!" said Pooh. "That's a part of Communication too! I remember that from learning how to be a V.I.B. (Very Important Bear) and a manager."

"That's right," said The Stranger. "And it serves the same purpose here, to allow you to monitor the progress of your solution as it is implemented, or Employed."

"Here it is! Here it is!" cried Piglet, jumping up and down frantically although the basket was still approaching the bridge, drifting lazily in the current.

"It doesn't seem right, somehow," said Pooh. "I think it is going to pass under the bridge toward that end."

"Very good, Pooh," said The Stranger. "Then let us adjust our solution, based on your feedback, and move over there."

The Stranger went to where the basket was likely to pass and got down and prepared to lean out with the stick in his hand to reach for the basket. Piglet and Pooh grabbed on to his legs to hold him steady, but The Stranger was much bigger than your average animal in the Forest, not to mention your average Piglet in the Forest, so it was not an easy thing. As the basket came closer, it started to swirl and spin from the currents next to the bridge.

"Wait," said The Stranger, "move a little left!"

Since he was upside down and even on the best of days was still confused about which was left and which was right, Pooh asked tentatively, "To the left?"

"Right."

"Right?" cried Pooh.

"No. To the left!"

"Help!" cried Piglet, who was holding fast to The Stranger's cuff but was being tossed to and fro for his trouble.

"A little farther out now!" cried The Stranger. "I've almost got it!"

"Is out left or right?" Pooh asked Piglet.

"Wait, no . . . just a little more . . . hold on, I'm starting to slip. . . ."

"It must be left, that sounds right," said Pooh.

"I'm slipping!" shouted The Stranger.

"I think he's feeding back," observed Piglet.

"Should we adjust something?" asked Pooh.

"Help! Help!" cried Piglet, who was losing his grip on The Stranger's cuff.

SPLASH!

"Is that what they call a Fallback?" asked Piglet as he

and Pooh stood by the railing and stared down at the river.

And with the splash, Rabbit and Roo came bounding out of the woods and ran up to where Pooh and Piglet were leaning over the railing, staring at where The Stranger had been only a moment before. "Can we help? We heard the shouting and came as quickly as we could."

The Stranger bobbed to the surface with the stick in one hand and the basket in his other.

"Should we start Hooshing?" shouted Pooh.

The Stranger didn't answer but waded to the bank.

Pooh and Piglet and Rabbit and Roo all hurried off the bridge and down to where The Stranger had come ashore, set the basket on a stump, and was shaking the water off his clothes.

They were all silent. No one was quite sure what The Stranger might do.

"I . . . uh . . . I'm sorry," stammered Pooh. "I thought we had a better grip. And then there was the shouting, and you said 'right,' and I thought you meant left, I mean, you said. . . ."

"That's all right, Pooh," said The Stranger. "One thing about solving problems, sometimes you get wet. But did you learn anything?"

"I learned something!" Piglet said, jumping up now that he saw that The Stranger wasn't going to get angry. "I learned that next time we do this, you should try to grab the basket without falling in."

"Thank you, Piglet."

"So, I guess we failed at solving the problem," said Pooh sadly.

"Well," said The Stranger, "what do you think? What was our goal?"

"To rescue the basket?" said Pooh.

"And did we?" asked The Stranger.

"Uh, yes . . ." said Pooh slowly.

"And how else did we say that we would judge our success?" asked The Stranger.

"Our cafeteria!" shouted Piglet, at which point Rabbit

and Roo cast glances at each other, not quite understanding what was going on.

"Criteria."

"We said," said Pooh, brightening, "that getting the basket out was one part . . . and that whether or not the food was wet was another," he said, the words coming faster as he realized, "and if it was wet, how much . . ." Pooh opened the top of the basket and began pawing through the contents.

"Success! We solved it!" he cried, and lifted a wet but intact jar of honey out of the basket. "The sandwiches and things were packed on top of this jar, and just like *The Floating Bear*, it must have floated and kept the basket up."

"So," said The Stranger, "based on what we said was the goal and the criteria against which we would measure our solution, this *was* a success."

"But you got all wet!" said Piglet.

"Yes, that's true," said The Stranger. "And next time, I'm going to make sure that one of the constraints is Not Getting Wet." The Stranger laughed and began to unload the picnic hamper while Piglet told Rabbit and Roo all about the adventure and how Pooh and he had solved the problem all by themselves.

Meanwhile, Pooh was not heard to say much of anything more than "Mmmmmmm, Hmmmmm," and "Hmmmmmmm, Mmmmmmm."

"But let's finish the story about the flood," said The Stranger when Piglet had come to the end of his explanation. "And you'll see that Pooh has some experience at testing things on a small scale, as he has done it before." And The Stranger told the rest of the tale.

"Now then, Pooh," said Christopher Robin, "where's your boat?"

"I ought to say," explained Pooh as they walked down to the shore of the island, "that it isn't just an ordinary sort of boat. Sometimes it's a Boat, and sometimes it's more of an Accident. It all depends."

"Depends on what?"

"On whether I'm on the top of it or underneath it."

"Oh! Well, where is it?"

"There!" said Pooh, pointing proudly to *The Floating Bear*.

It wasn't what Christopher Robin expected, and the more he looked at it, the more he thought what a Brave and Clever Bear Pooh was, and the more Christopher Robin thought this, the more Pooh looked modestly down his nose and tried to pretend he wasn't.

"But it's too small for two of us," said Christopher Robin sadly.

"Three of us with Piglet."

"That makes it smaller still. Oh, Pooh Bear, what shall we do?"

And then this Bear, Pooh Bear, Winnie-the-Pooh, F.O.P. (Friend of Piglet's), R.C. (Rabbit's Companion), P.D. (Pole Discoverer), E.C. and T.F. (Eeyore's Comforter and Tail-Finder)—in fact, Pooh himself—said something so clever that Christopher Robin could only look at him with mouth open and eyes staring, wondering if this was really the Bear of Very Little Brain whom he had known and loved so long.

"We might go in your umbrella," said Pooh.

"?"

"We might go in your umbrella," said Pooh.

"??"

"We might go in your umbrella," said Pooh.

"!!!!!!"

For suddenly Christopher Robin saw that they might. He opened his umbrella and put it point downwards in the water. It floated but wobbled. Pooh got in. He was just beginning to say that it was all right now, when he found that it wasn't, so after a short drink which he didn't really want he waded back to Christopher Robin. Then they both got in together, and it wobbled no longer.

"I shall call this boat *The Brain of Pooh*," said Christopher Robin, and *The Brain of Pooh* set sail forthwith in a south-westerly direction, revolving gracefully.

You can imagine [Piglet's] joy when at last he saw the good ship, *The Brain of Pooh* (*Captain*, C. Robin; *1st Mate*, P. Bear) coming over the sea to rescue him.

"So *The Brain of Pooh* was your solution to how to rescue Piglet," said The Stranger. "And having chosen that solution, you went about testing it by getting inside and trying it out before you and Christopher Robin committed yourselves to setting off in search of Piglet."

"And a good thing too," said Pooh. "I found that the umbrella was quite tippy, unless of course you had *both* a captain and a first mate on board."

"And that's just the type of thing that testing on a small scale can do for you when you are using it to try and solve a problem."

So they ate their lunch, and Pooh, having finished his honey, and before starting on some bread with condensed milk, sang his Problem-Solving Rhyme, and even added a last verse:

> *Employ the best idea found,*
> *And watch what happens most precisely,*
> *Making sure by looking round,*
> *That things are working out quite nicely.*

After they had finished, The Stranger got up and thanked Pooh and Piglet for their help but said he had to leave as he was still quite wet and needed to go home and change before he got the wheezles and sneezles.

"But before I go," said The Stranger, "I'd like to review what we talked about regarding the final step in the Problem-Solving Method: Employ the Solution and Monitor Results. That having Visualized and Selected a Solution in the previous step, we begin by Creating an Action Plan."

"Which is another way of saying 'creating a path from here to there,'" said Piglet to Roo in exactly the tone of voice he had heard used when he rode in Christopher Robin's pocket and went to school.

"That's right," said The Stranger. "And the next part is Testing on a Small Scale, where we try out the solution in a small way to see how well it works. We do this by defining exactly what success is and developing criteria . . ."

"That's like a yardstick," Pooh whispered to Rabbit, "for measuring."

". . . that we use to judge our relative success. We make changes in our solution as they are warranted while we are Employing it, and we try to have a fallback option in case things go wrong."

"Although falling back in the water is Not Desired," said Pooh.

"So true, Pooh," said The Stranger. "Once we have tested successfully on a small scale, we use the same process to Employ our Solution full scale, and we continue to Monitor the Results, being alert for any feedback that would indicate a change might be necessary. If you have followed all of the steps to this point, your solution will be Employed easily, and your problem will be solved."

"Hence, you have lunch," said Pooh proudly.

IX

IN WHICH The Stranger Takes Everyone on an Adventure, Piglet Finds a Fair-sized Problem, and Pooh SOLVEs It

"The Fair! The Fair!" squeaked Piglet, scurrying ahead of the others toward the entrance booth, with Roo trailing slightly behind crying "Oh! Oh!" and acting Very Excited.

"It will rain," said Eeyore, looking up at the cloudless sky. "Sun in the morning; rain without warning. That's what they say."

"Thank you very much for bringing us," said Pooh to The Stranger.

"Not at all, Pooh," said The Stranger. "It is the least I could do, since all of you have helped me so much with my work. And going to a Country Fair is one of my favorite things to do."

"Tiggers like fairs best," said Tigger.

"And I shall enjoy the exhibitions," said Owl. "Did I ever tell you about the time that my great uncle Horace won the blue ribbon at a fair for Best of Show? It was during the fall of the Rainy Year . . ."

While The Stranger went to buy tickets, the others listened to Owl, and Pooh stared with wonder at the fair. The Stranger had heard about the pageant and fair that was being held in a clearing near the village, on the other side of the Forest from the Hundred Acre Wood. He had invited everyone to join him for an afternoon. They waited for The Stranger to return with the tickets and stared at the brightly colored tents, banners, and flags. At the center of the small grouping of tents was a gently turning Ferris wheel. It was almost as tall as the Bee Tree. They watched as the wheel swung lazily around, and listened to the music from the wheel drifting across the fairgrounds.

Tigger went off in search of whatever it is Tiggers like best at fairs, and Owl and Eeyore went to one of the tents. Pooh, Piglet, Rabbit, Roo, and The Stranger walked along, taking in the sights and sounds of the fair.

"I think I shall get some popcorn," said The Stranger. "Would you like anything, Pooh? Piglet? Rabbit? Roo?"

"No, thank you," said Rabbit. "I am going to ride the Ferris wheel, and I shall want to have my hands free."

"Me too!" said Roo.

"All right," said The Stranger. "We'll meet at the Ferris wheel."

And The Stranger walked off toward the concession stand.

"Would you like to come with us, Pooh?" asked Rabbit.

"No, thank you," said Pooh. "I have been thinking of a hum about the fair, and I think I shall stay here and hum it until it is fully Thought."

"What about you, Piglet?"

Piglet looked at the wheel. It looked very high.

"No," he said. "I think I'll stay with Pooh in case he needs help with his hum."

Roo and Rabbit hurried off toward the Ferris wheel.

"Wave to us when you get up to the very top!" Pooh called after them.

"We shall," Roo squeaked.

Pooh and Piglet sat down on a bench and watched the people walk by while Pooh thought of his hum and waited for The Stranger to return. Piglet noticed that Rabbit and Roo were on the Ferris wheel at the very top, and he could just make out the two tiny figures sitting in the seat, waving and waving. Piglet waved back.

Pooh waited for more of his hum to come to him. When he looked up, he too noticed that Rabbit and Roo were at the very top of the wheel and were waving at him. He waved back.

Pooh thought he saw The Stranger returning from the concession stand, but it turned out to be someone else.

Piglet looked up again, and Rabbit and Roo were *still* at the very top of the wheel and were waving just as hard as before. They must be having a grand time he thought, and he continued to watch, wanting to see the wheel as it turned round.

But the wheel did not turn.

Rabbit and Roo continued to wave and wave. Piglet thought this was Very Strange. Usually Ferris wheels went around and around all the time. Or at least that was his impression from what Christopher Robin had told him. But as he watched, the Ferris wheel did not move, and Rabbit and Roo continued to be in the seat at the very top of the wheel and continued to wave and wave their arms. Piglet decided to go see.

"Pooh? I think I may have found a problem," said Piglet.

"And what is that, Piglet?" said Pooh.

"Come with me to the Ferris wheel and we shall see," said Piglet.

As Piglet and Pooh made their way toward the Ferris wheel, Tigger came bouncing up to them. "Pooh! Piglet! Come quick! The Ferris wheel is stuck and Rabbit and Roo are on it, so they have become stuck as well!" So with Tigger leading the way through the crowd, Pooh and Piglet hurried to the wheel.

When they arrived, the wheel operator was standing next to the control lever that started and stopped the wheel, looking up, and wiping his brow with a handkerchief.

"What has happened?" asked Pooh.

"I don't know," said the operator. "Everything was working fine, and then all of a sudden the gears jammed, and it stopped."

Pooh looked up and could see Rabbit and Roo in the seat at the very top of the wheel, rocking back and forth as they waved and waved their arms. He couldn't quite hear what they were calling, if they were calling at all. Perhaps they weren't worried yet, thinking that this must just be part of Riding a Ferris wheel.

"Don't worry," Piglet called up to the pair, just in case they knew they were stuck. "We'll get you down," he added, though he wasn't quite sure how just yet. But it was always helpful to be comforting.

Just then, Owl and Eeyore rushed up following Tigger, who had gone to fetch them.

"What . . . what has happened?" asked Owl, gasping from the hurry.

"Rabbit and Roo have become stuck at the top of the Ferris wheel!" said Pooh. "This is a problem."

"I knew it," said Eeyore gloomily. "I knew it was too good to be true. I should have known it was the kind of day for a problem."

"Is there anything you can do?" asked Pooh of the operator.

"Not until they send someone to repair it. It could take hours," said the operator. "Lucky that only your friends were on at the time. I was just about to load some more people when it stopped."

Pooh didn't know why the operator thought it was lucky that Rabbit and Roo were stuck, as it didn't seem to be the kind of thing that Pooh thought was lucky at all.

"They do seem," said Owl, "to be ensconced in an unreachable aerie, at the zenith of this cyclical transport."

"And they're stuck at the top of the ride too," said Tigger.

"So we must rescue them," said Pooh firmly. "This is a problem, and we shall SOLVE it!"

"What do we do first?" asked Tigger, who, because of his bounciness during the many discussions on Problem Solving with The Stranger, hadn't paid proper attention, and so was quite unsure where to start.

"The first step," said Pooh confidently, "is to Select the Problem. The S step from SOLVE."

"It seems that the problem—" Eeyore started to say.

"—selected us," finished Piglet excitedly.

Pooh began to hum his problem-solving hum to himself. When he got to the second verse he said slowly, "The next step is to Observe. . . . Observe, Organize, and Define the Problem. Just *What* is the problem?"

"The problem is," said Owl, "that Rabbit and Roo are entrapped at the top!"

"And the wheel can't move," added Tigger.

"And it doesn't look good," said Eeyore.

"It will be hours," said Piglet, squeaking faster and faster, "before they are able to get a repair crew here to fix it, and both Rabbit and Roo are Very Excitable. I don't think that they will be very happy when they realize what has happened. We *must* find a way to get them down."

"Without falling," said Tigger. "That's a constraint, remember?"

"Good," said Pooh, wishing he weren't a Bear of Very Little Brain, and hoping he had learned enough about solving problems. "And what are we starting with?"

"We have everything one might have," said Owl, "if he were at a Country Fair."

"And there are all of us," said Tigger. He looked around and some people were looking up and pointing at the two very small figures in the seat at the very top of the wheel, waving their arms and rocking their seat back and forth.

"So what shall we do next?" asked Eeyore. "Not that it likely will do any good, but I suppose we should try."

"The next step is to Learn by Questioning," said Pooh. "We must ask the five W's and How? in the right order, and try to understand more about the problem. Does anyone remember the correct order?" Pooh stared at the blank faces before him. "Let me think."

Pooh thought for a good long minute. Actually, he hummed. He hummed to himself the next verse of his Problem-Solving Hum, remembering that when he had made it up, he had been very careful about the order of the five W's and How so that he would always remember them. Like now.

> *Learn all you can by asking a lot,*
> *But in the right order, as they are now,*
> *Mostly Whys and then some Whats,*
> *Then Where and When and Who and How.*
>
> *(And after each, ask Why again.)*

"I have it," said Pooh. And he explained the five W's and How? to the others in the correct order so that they could help him. "We know the Why of the problem, as we want to get Rabbit and Roo down safely because they are our friends. So let's start with the What."

"What is keeping the wheel from moving?" asked Eeyore.

They all looked at the operator. "The gears have jammed," he said.

"And Why?" asked Pooh, remembering that this was always a good question to ask, no matter what.

"I think because the drive belt broke and pieces of it fell in between the gears," said the operator.

The animals all looked at one another. None of them, except Owl of course, knew anything at all about gears and drive belts, and at this point Owl was being quiet as he wanted to be quite sure before he said anything.

"Is there a way to make it move without the motor?" asked Tigger.

"Very good, Tigger," said Pooh.

"I don't think so," said the operator. "The automatic brake has engaged and until we fix the motor and the gears, we won't be able to move the wheel."

"Oh," they all said.

Pooh stepped back and looked up at the top of the wheel. Rabbit and Roo were still waving their arms and rocking back and forth.

"Where is. The Stranger?" asked Pooh, looking back toward the concession stand where he had last seen him. "I do wish he were here to help. *He* would know what to do."

"Ahem! In previous occurrences of this type, that is *When* this happened before, what did you do?" asked Owl. Pooh was pleased that Owl had asked a When question, and just at the right time.

"Mostly we just waited for the repair crew," said the operator. "When the people were finally able to get off, we tried to make it up to them by offering them free rides, but not many usually took them."

"I'm not surprised," said Eeyore.

"Who can fix the wheel?" asked Pooh. "And how do they do it?"

"I don't know," said the operator.

"Why do they leave the people on while they fix it?" Tigger asked.

"I don't think they do," said the operator. "They usually get them off first so that there's no load on the motor."

"But how do they do that?" asked Piglet. "And can we do that now?"

"I wish we could," said the operator, "but you see, the repair crew has a special tool they use . . ." and on and on he went talking about extension ladders, flywheels, and centrifugal brakes and other things that Pooh was sure he didn't know the least thing about.

Finally, the operator finished his explanation and Owl nodded wisely as though he had understood.

"So," asked Pooh, "can you get them down?"

"No," said the operator.

"Just as I thought," said Eeyore.

"I too," said Owl. "An irreducible conundrum, with a dearth of expeditious alternatives."

"Well, we did find out that the wheel won't move," said Pooh, looking about again for The Stranger and wishing he were there. "Tigger? Would you be so kind as to bounce off and search for The Stranger? I think he could help us a great deal, but it seems that he has misplaced himself."

"Tiggers are good at finding people. Especially at a Fair," said Tigger. He bounded off with a "Worraworra-worraworra."

"Now let me see," said Pooh. "We have arrived at the

point where we know about the problem and must Visualize Possible Solutions, Select One, and Refine It. . . . Do any of you have any thoughts? Oh, I wish Christopher Robin were here. I always seem to have much better thoughts when he is around."

"Why don't you just ask Owl to fly up to the top of the Ferris wheel and bring them down?" asked Eeyore. "The simplest thing. I should have thought of it sooner, but I was thinking about the rain, which will be coming down any minute now."

"Ahem," said Owl, preparing to give his now well-practiced speech on the Necessary Dorsal Muscles, when Pooh interrupted.

"That's a good idea, Eeyore. Do you have any more?" said Pooh. "The more ideas we have, the better our chance of success."

"I shan't be able to rescue Rabbit," said Owl, "but I might be able to help Roo, who is quite a bit smaller and not so much a strain on the Necessary Dors—"

"Another idea!" exclaimed Pooh. "Very good. Things are beginning to look up!" At which point Eeyore and Owl looked up, for this was what they thought Pooh had wanted, and when Tigger bounced up, he too looked up.

"Tigger, did you find The Stranger?" asked Pooh.

"Finding strangers is what Tiggers do best," he said. "But Tiggers do much better finding strangers in the woods, where there aren't so many strangers about."

"We shall just have to come up with more ideas ourselves," said Pooh. "What if we tried something that has helped rescue someone before?"

"Like a note in a bottle?" asked Piglet.

"We could try standing on one another's shoulders. Except for the fact that it might snap my back in two, because naturally I'd be on the bottom," said Eeyore.

"If Christopher Robin were here, we could use his tunic and let Rabbit and Roo jump into it," said Tigger.

"That would never work," said Eeyore. "They're much too high."

"Now, Eeyore," said Pooh gently, "when we are thinking of ideas, it is important that we remember the rule that we not criticize them right away. Because even bad ideas might remind us of good ones and we don't want to lose any good ones, remember?" Tigger felt better because it had been his idea, and Eeyore felt worse because he had been corrected, but then he had expected it.

"I'm out of ideas, Pooh," said Piglet.

"Well, then," said Pooh, "we should try those techniques that The Stranger taught us to get more ideas. Let's see . . . the first one was . . . make it bigger . . . I think."

"If the Ferris wheel were bigger," said Piglet, "I think we should never get them down."

"And if they were bigger," said Eeyore, "the wheel would snap like a donkey's back and they *would* be down."

· "I don't think this is working so well," said Piglet.

"We must give it time," said Pooh. "Now the next thing was to make something smaller."

"If the wheel were smaller," said Eeyore, "that would be the same as if they were bigger. No help at all."

"And if they were smaller," said Tigger, "they could crawl down all by themselves."

"Could they really do that?" said Pooh.

"Ants do," said Tigger. "Climb trees, that is."

"But do you think," said Pooh, looking up again at the two small figures, "that they might be able to climb down themselves?"

"I don't think Roos are built for climbing," said Piglet.

"Or Rabbits," said Tigger.

"Or Donkeys," said Eeyore.

"Then we must continue thinking of ideas," said Pooh. "The next technique, I think, was to reverse something."

"If we could reverse the wheel, we could bring them right down," said Piglet. "But the operator said we couldn't."

"I think what The Stranger meant," said Piglet, "is that we reverse one part of the problem, like . . ."

"Like figuring out how to get Rabbit and Roo up there," said Eeyore, "instead of trying to get them down."

"Exactly," said Pooh.

"That gives me an idea!" shouted Piglet. "Remember

during the Great Blusterous Day? When we went to visit Owl and his house decided to reverse itself?"

"Of course," said Owl. "There is nothing wrong with my memory. Tell me about it again. The parts that interest you, of course."

"The house was upside down," Piglet explained, talking faster and faster as he went on, from excitement, "and the door was on the ceiling, and we had to get out, and we didn't know quite how we would do it, and I was small but Owl's Necessary Dorsal Muscles were the same as they are now and the letter-box was small and so we sent Owl up with the string and then pulled me up to get Christopher Robin."

Piglet stood panting, expectantly waiting for a response. "Don't you see, what if we were to put a string up to the top of the wheel? Then we could tie it to me and pull me up and . . . Oh. I guess that wouldn't work after all. It would just get me stuck up there with them."

"Lowering," said Eeyore.

"Yes, that's it!" said Piglet. "What if we used the string for *lowering* Rabbit and Roo, instead of raising them like they did with me?"

"No," said Eeyore. "I meant the skies are lowering. I think it's going to rain after all."

"Still," said Pooh, "that's a Very Good Idea, Piglet."

Piglet felt especially proud, for not only had he had a Very Good Idea, but he wouldn't have to be tied to a string and raised up very high. Which he remembered, but not fondly.

"And that is the Best Idea yet," said Pooh. "Tell us again, Piglet, so that we can Refine and Improve It."

"I just thought . . . I mean, if we could just . . ." Piglet stammered, stopped, and then started all over again after taking a deep breath. "My Very Good Idea is that we should get a string and use it for lowering Rabbit and Roo from the top of the Ferris wheel in just the opposite way that I was raised to the letter box."

"That *is* a Very Good Plan," said Pooh after a moment's reflection. "But I'm still having trouble with the Hows. How do we get the string up there, and How do we lower them, and How . . ."

"We shall need to get a very long piece of string," said Piglet. "And we shall need to have Owl fly it up to the top of the wheel. And we shall need to loop it over, and we shall need him to explain our Plan to Rabbit and Roo."

"That is an improvement," said Owl.

"And we must hurry!" Pooh said.

"Before it rains," said Eeyore.

Pooh looked up and noticed that the two very small figures in the seat at the very top of the Ferris wheel had stopped waving and rocking and were just sitting there.

"The next step is . . ." And here Pooh paused and tried hard to remember just what it was that was the next step, and surprised even himself, a Bear of Very Little Brain, when he said, "Employ the Solution and Monitor Results! The last step of the SOLVE Problem-Solving Method."

"Oh, boy!" said Piglet. "We need an Action Plan!"

"Action Plans are what Tiggers do best," said Tigger. "What's an Action Plan?"

"It's a plan of action," said Owl.

"Oh."

"We shall need some string," said Eeyore. "Waterproof, preferably."

"And we shall have to test it," said Piglet, remembering how they had tested the string when The Stranger's briefcase had fallen into the Very Deep Pit.

"And we shall have to think about what to tell Rabbit and Roo when I fly up there," said Owl.

"This is a Very Good Action Plan," said Pooh. "Let's begin. Tigger, can you go find a very long piece of string?"

"Finding string is what Tiggers do best," and he bounced off toward the midway.

Within moments he was back to the surprise of all with a large bobbin of string that he had found, saying that he had explained the problem to the balloon man, who had offered to help by giving him the whole ball of balloon string.

"Pooh?" said Piglet. "I think I have found a constraint."

"What is that?" said Pooh.

"It is a thing which keeps you from doing something," said Piglet.

"No, no, I know that," said Pooh. "I mean, what is the constraint that you have found?"

"I don't think that string will hold them," said Piglet.

"At least not Rabbit, who is much larger than I, although it may hold Roo, who is much smaller than I."

Pooh thought for a moment. "Then we shall have to try it on a small scale first. To see if it works." So Pooh led the others over to a tent and tied the string to a small scale they found there. It was just about the size of Roo, but because it was made of metal was about as heavy as Piglet, and with all of them pulling together, they tried to lift it. *Snap!* The string broke.

"Like a Donkey's back," said Eeyore.

"You were right, Piglet," said Pooh. "Now we shall have to try something else."

"If we made it bigger," said Owl, "the string, that is, it would be just fine."

"Perhaps," said Pooh, "we can tie a large piece of rope to the end of our string, and then pull it up to them once the string is there."

"I think we'd better go find a piece of rope," said Eeyore to Tigger, "before it starts to rain." And the two of them rushed off.

"Our Plan hasn't changed, has it, Pooh?" asked Piglet anxiously. He hoped it was still a Very Good Idea Piglet Plan.

"Not really," said Pooh. "We are just carrying out the refining and improving step."

"Is there anything we can do while we're waiting?" said Piglet.

"Owl? Can you fly the end of this string up to Rabbit and Roo and explain to them what our Plan is?"

"Certainly," said Owl, and he took the end of the string and began to fly up to the very top of the Ferris wheel.

He flew up and up, and as he got higher the string got longer and longer and heavier and heavier until, when he was very near the top, he had stopped flying up and was . . . stopped. Flying but stopped.

"What's happening?" squeaked Piglet.

"I think Owl is having trouble getting all the way to the top of the wheel," said Pooh.

"Well, he makes a very splendid kite," said Piglet, watching as Owl stopped flapping, and turned and glided down to land in front of them.

"I think . . . *puff* . . . *puff* . . . that the string . . . *puff* . . . *puff* . . . is too heavy . . . *puff* . . . *puff*. Necessary . . . *puff* . . . *puff* . . . Dorsal . . . *puff* . . . *puff* . . . Muscles . . . *puff* . . . *puff* . . . you know . . . *puff* . . . *puff*."

"Oh, Bother!" said Pooh. "Problems, problems, problems." And he sat down and tried to think. At that moment, Tigger bounced up, and Eeyore followed a moment later with a length of rope coiled on top of his back.

"We've found the rope!" bounced Tigger.

"And it's dry," said Eeyore, "though it won't be for long."

"We have another problem," said Piglet. "Owl cannot fly the string up to the top of the wheel because his Necessary Dorsal Muscles aren't enough so we can't get the string up to the top, so we can't tie the rope to it, so we can't pull the rope up, so we can't tie the rope to Rabbit and Roo and lower them down and rescue them!"

They all looked up again to the top of the wheel, where they saw the small figures again rocking and waving in the small seat. Several seagulls had perched on the top of the motionless wheel, and were sitting and staring at the curious pair.

"A kite!" shouted Pooh.

"Looks more like gulls to me," said Eeyore, squinting into the sun.

"No, no. I mean, perhaps we can use a kite to get the string up to them," said Pooh.

"That's a Very Good Idea, Pooh," said Piglet. "However did you think of it?"

"Well, I was thinking about changing plans on the fly, and that flies are much too small to be helpful with this, and then remembering when you said Owl looked like a kite up there, and then I thought about flying a kite, and how the string goes all the way up to the kite, much higher than the top of the wheel, and that's how I thought it . . . I think."

"Will it work?" asked Piglet. "Will it still be my 'Very Good Idea'?"

"Of course," said Pooh. "You had the original idea."

"Do we know where there's a kite?" asked Piglet.

"No."

"Oh."

I wish The Stranger would get back soon," said Pooh. "Perhaps he would know how to build a kite, or maybe where to find one."

"Maybe we can send up some balloons," said Piglet. "Like the time that you went after the honey in the honey tree. And then if Christopher Robin were here with his gun, he could shoot out the balloons and down they would drop."

"Too high," said Eeyore. "Much too high for Rabbit and Roo to drop, that is."

"But not if they were Jagulars," said Piglet, "who are Very Good Droppers."

"That's it!" said Pooh. "We shall do it!"

"Turn them into Jagulars?" said Tigger.

"No. Piglet has given me a Very Good Idea," said Pooh. "We shall make a kite out of balloons. We can tie one end of the string to the balloons and fly them up like a kite until they reach Rabbit and Roo. Then, they can grab the string and pull up the rope. And finally they can tie themselves to the rope and we'll all lower them down!"

It was very quiet as they all thought about Pooh's plan. It sounded like a Very Complex Plan when you heard it all at once, but each part of it had seemed so simple before. So surely it should work.

"Congratulations, Pooh!" said Piglet. "It is a Wonderful Plan."

So while Tigger went back to the balloon man to get some balloons for the kite, Owl flew up to Rabbit and Roo to explain the Plan, and Piglet and Pooh tied the string to the end of the rope. By now a small crowd of children had gathered around the base of the Ferris wheel and were watching them prepare their rescue. Tigger returned, bouncing even higher than usual due to the large bunch of balloons he was holding with one paw.

"Getting balloons is what Tiggers do best," he said.

"Now hold still, Tigger," said Piglet, "while I tie the balloons to the string."

Owl flew back down and landed lightly beside them.

"Are they ready?" asked Pooh. "And do they understand what they are to do?"

"They are currently resident in a state of high vigilance and anticipation," said Owl.

"Does that mean yes?" Pooh whispered to Piglet.

"It doesn't matter," said Eeyore, who had overheard. "We'd better try now anyway, before it starts to rain."

And their Plan worked just as they had thought.

Well, not quite. The balloons floated up in the breeze, just like a kite, but it was only after getting the knack of where the wind was coming from, that and unwrapping them from the odd tree or two, that they were able to get the string up to Rabbit and Roo. From then on the Plan worked just as they had thought.

Well, not quite. Rabbit forgot the part about untying the string from the balloons before they pulled the rope up, and Roo forgot the part about letting go of the string while they were pulling, so that they wound up with the rope halfway to the top of the wheel, and Roo halfway between Rabbit and the balloons, and the balloons halfway to the Forest before they noticed. Of course, after they got Roo down, and untied the balloons and pulled the rope up, from *then* on, the Plan worked just as they had thought.

Well, not quite. Eeyore wanted to be the anchor when they began to lower Rabbit and Roo, and so had asked Pooh to tie the rope to him so that he could walk slowly toward the wheel while the others held on and Rabbit and Roo were lowered to the ground. When Rabbit and Roo finally touched the ground, a cheer went up from the on-lookers who had gathered to watch the rescue.

Pooh and Piglet and Owl and Tigger let go of the rope and rushed over to meet them, and Eeyore, knowing the Rescue was over, wandered off toward the other tents. He had forgotten to undo the rope, and a moment later, Rabbit and Roo were lifted abruptly above their friends, and continued to rise, swinging back and forth until Piglet was able to convince Eeyore he should return. From *then* on, everything went just as they had thought.

Everyone praised Rabbit and Roo for their bravery, and Owl for his flying, Tigger for his finding and Eeyore for his pulling, and Piglet for his stopping Eeyore's pulling and his Very Good Idea. But most of all, they congratulated Pooh and one another for their Problem Solving by using SOLVE successfully.

The operator thanked them for getting Rabbit and Roo down from the top of the Ferris wheel and told them that when the repair crew had finished their work, they could come back and take all the free rides they wanted, although none of them except Roo really wanted to.

And when the onlookers began to drift away to ride the rides and see the sights, The Stranger returned.

"Is there a problem here?" asked The Stranger, carrying some popcorn and some other treats.

"No," said Pooh. "No problem at all."

X

IN WHICH the Problem-Solving Song Is Paraded and The Stranger Returns Home

Work on the Problem-Solving Book was finished, except for Writing It All Down, and The Stranger was leaving the Forest to begin that part of making a book.

Pooh felt that they should do the Customary and Proper thing.

"Piglet," Pooh said firmly, "we shall have a parade and music before The Stranger leaves."

So Pooh and Piglet got busy.

It was decided to have Rabbit organize the parade since he was used to coping with a large number of his smaller friends-and-relations and arranging them in a line so that they wouldn't get stepped on, which was pretty much the idea of a parade, according to Owl.

Rabbit agreed and after he got everyone's place properly set in his mind he gathered them all in a circle and told them exactly what each was to do.

Pooh, since he liked to make up songs, was in charge of the music part of the Celebration. He rehearsed everyone carefully until each knew his individual part and all could begin and end the music at the same time, or close enough so that it didn't matter. Even Eeyore, who was a Basso Profundo, thought the music was very good and appropriate for the beginning of an Important thing.

"Unless it rains," he said. "Then some lose their voices or get wheezles and sneezles in the middle of a note."

They had agreed to meet The Stranger at the edge of the Hundred Acre Wood before he left. Everyone from the Forest was there early: Pooh, Piglet, Rabbit, Tigger, Eeyore, Kanga, Roo, Small, and almost all of Rabbit's smaller friends-and-relations.

When The Stranger came along, the parade was all organized, and Rabbit gave the signal to start. It went very well with only a few minor problems like a collision in midair between Tigger and Kanga due to Tigger being carried away by the parade and being unable to restrain his bounciness.

Also Rabbit's smaller friends-and-relations tended to bunch up toward the end of the parade, and several times Eeyore had to warn Small about being stepped on, but afterward everyone agreed that it had undoubtedly been one of the finest parades ever held in the Hundred Acre Wood and certainly just as good as the one at the Fair.

At the end of the parade Pooh had instructed everyone to take their positions in the chorus for the music part of the Celebration. Piglet, Small, and most of Rabbit's smaller friends-and-relations were in the very front row, as they had the highest voices, and Eeyore was all alone in the back row, since he had the deepest voice.

Pooh stood out in front to lead because he knew the song best, having written it. He raised his arms and then brought them down, and almost everyone started to sing Pooh's Problem-Solving Song for The Stranger.

Select the problem of the day,
Finding one that's right to do,
You can choose it either way,
You pick it or it picks you.

Observe it very carefully,
"Where do I start? Where am I going?"
And don't forget about the bee,
"What's in the way of doing or knowing?"

Learn all you can by asking a lot,
But in the right order, as they are now,
Mostly Whys and then some Whats,
Then Where and When and Who and How.

(And after each, ask Why again.)

Vis-u-a-lize ideas, of course,
We think our thoughts and hope that they
Will put the cart behind the horse,
And not around the other way.

Employ the best idea found,
And watch what happens most precisely,
Making sure by looking 'round,
That things are working out quite nicely.

And for once, everybody, even Eeyore and Small, finished at the same time, and there was an echo which came back from the Hundred Acre Wood to add exactly the right touch.

There was silence for a moment and then The Stranger

was applauding and Pooh bowed and then applauded the chorus and soon everybody was applauding one another and then it was time to spread a blanket out and have lunch.

After lunch, the blanket that had been spread on the ground to eat lunch on was carefully cleaned of crumbs, inspected to make sure that none of Small's relatives were still clinging to it, and then folded away into The Stranger's basket.

First, of course, Pooh, being a Very Helpful Bear, had checked inside the basket to be certain that there was not the odd forgotten pot of honey or some of the little cake things with pink sugar icing there to make the basket heavier to carry than it had to be.

Finally, all the Good-byes had been said and then said again, just to make certain that everyone had his chance. The Thank-yous were very nicely offered and Good Lucks and Best Wishes were returned. Then it could not be put off any longer. They watched The Stranger walk away. He turned and waved one last time, disappearing into the trees.

They all waved back, except for Small and some of his relatives, who were so close to the ground that they had lost sight of The Stranger long ago. Besides, Small and some of his relatives were not properly shaped for waving, having six legs, and trying to decide which one to wave with caused them to become confused and fall about.

They all waited until the setting sun had almost sunk

behind the trees so that they were sure The Stranger was well on his way. Then the gathering slowly dispersed.

Pooh and Piglet walked home thoughtfully together in the golden evening, and for a long time they were silent.

"When you wake up in the morning, Pooh," said Piglet at last, "what's the first thing you say to yourself?"

"What's for breakfast?" said Pooh. "What do *you* say, Piglet?"

"I say I wonder what's going to happen exciting *today*?" said Piglet.

Pooh nodded thoughtfully.

"It's the same thing," he said.

Almost the first thing The Stranger did upon returning home was sit down and relax in the comfortable armchair that was just the right distance from the Very Nice Fire burning on the hearth. The first thing, of course, had been to light the fire, the wood having been properly arranged in the fireplace, ready for lighting.

Tomorrow, it would be necessary to begin the actual writing of *Winnie-the-Pooh on Problem Solving*, but now it was nice just to sit down without having to check whether one was sitting on a gorse bush or a thistle or Small or Alexander Beetle. That was a problem in the Forest, but not here.

However, there was one thing that was certain. There was no lack of problems outside the Forest that needed to be solved. One was constantly bombarded by them in the media.

There were the big problems affecting almost everyone in the world. For the most part they stemmed from wars, revolutions, disasters, disease, and social, cultural, and environmental change.

There were always many small Problems that were important primarily to the individuals trying to deal with their consequences. These were the stuff of talk shows, advice columns, and the thousands of how-to books.

Many problems were old ones that either had never been solved satisfactorily or had been solved in the past but had returned in a new form due to changing circumstances or conditions and needed to be solved again.

Some were brand-new problems, never before encountered by humanity.

Finding solutions to some of them was demonstrably a matter of Life or Death. In other cases the consequences were not as serious; failure to find a solution would only result in annoyance or inconvenience.

It is quite likely that most of these problems can be successfully solved using the methods presented in this book.

What is needed are more individuals who want to find solutions for problems, who can do it effectively, and who like the challenge. Those individuals could make things better, for themselves and for the world.

The Stranger thought about Winnie-the-Pooh, Piglet, Owl, Tigger, and the others in the Forest who had helped with the book and had grasped the idea of using the SOLVE Problem-Solving Method. They had demonstrated that at the Fair and had shown that they could apply it and use it on their own. The Stranger was pleased about that. If a bear and his friends could do that, almost anyone could.

All you need to do is learn the SOLVE Method and practice it on the problems that you select or that select you. Before long, you can say confidently as Pooh did:

"No. No problem at all."

POOH'S APPENDIX
Winnie-the-Pooh's
Problem-SOLVE-ing Checklist

Pooh is sometimes a Very Forgetful Bear, so he uses this. In case you are forgetful too (or you want to make certain you don't miss any steps using the SOLVE Method), he very nicely says you may use it also.

Select the Problem or Situation

- ☐ I selected It
- ☐ It selected me
- ☐ Chosen to Improve
  a process or situation
- ☐ Simple
- ☐ Complex
- ☐ Single
- ☐ Multiple

Emotional associations (if yes, characterize) Y or N
State the problem or situation as clearly and simply as you can

Observe, Organize, and Define the Problem or Situation

Starting place (any initial conditions, resources, current status)
Goal (desired end result upon successful completion)
Constraints (any limiting factors or obstacles)

Learn by Questioning All Parts of the Problem

Why solve it?	Why is it a problem?
What specifically is the problem?	
Where does the problem occur?	Why does it occur there?
When does the problem occur?	Why does it occur then?
Who is involved?	Why are they involved?
How does it happen?	Why does it happen that way?

Visualize Possible Solutions, Select One, and Refine It

Experience—Have you ever had a similar problem? How was that solved?

Approach:

- ❏ Numerical—numbers
- ❏ Graphical—pics, graphs, diagrams
- ❏ Logical—logic, deduction, inference
- ❏ Analogy—similar item, process, idea
- ❏ Intuitive—gut feeling, hunch
- ❏ Other

Idea Generators—Use to generate ideas *without* qualifying or judging them. Take the problem or a part of it and:

Make it bigger	Remove something
Make it smaller	Replace something with something else
Add something	Combine two elements
Take something away	Free association (say anything and see what comes to mind)
Exchange two parts	

Choose best solution—*Now*, be judgmental and review all ideas for the best one, list pluses and minuses for each, and feel free to combine, or modify.

Refine and improve—Review the selected idea carefully and improve or tweak.

Employ the Solution and Monitor Results

Action Plan—Create a path from here to there—list of all the things that need to be accomplished or gathered in sequence with timing and responsibilities noted.

Test on a small scale—If applicable, try out your solution a little at a time.

Employ and monitor—Put solution in place, and monitor criteria that will indicate success.

! If at last, the solution does not work, take heart—you may have received a very large and negative feedback, but you are still in the process of solving; just repeat all the above steps using what you now know as additional input.

By the same authors. To be published August 1998.

Winnie-the-Pooh on Success
Roger E. Allen and Stephen D. Allen
With original line drawings by E.H. Shepard

What is Success? How do you achieve it? Who is successful? For Pooh, it is as simple as acquiring more honey, but in these complicated times, people from corporate managers to enrepreneurs and authors, have all sorts of different ideas about what it is to be successful.

Whatever your notion of success is, this book will help you to attain your goals. With the help of Winnie-the-Pooh, Piglet, Eeyore and the other members of the Hundred Acre Wood,the authors of *Winnie-the-Pooh on Management* and *Winnie-the-Pooh on Problem Solving*, and now *Winnie-the-Pooh on Success* set out to give you the tools that you need to be successful at any endeavor you choose.

Roger E. Allen and Stephen D. Allen are associates of Allen Associates, a USA based management consulting firm whose clients include organisations in the fields of public administrations, computers, finance, textiles and more. Both live in Washington.

The
Wisdom
of
Pooh

The Prestigious List from Methuen

"The Wisdom of Pooh range proves beyond all reasonable doubt, what
even Winnie-the-Pooh's most ardent fans may have hitherto underestimated,
yet many will have long suspected; that indeed Pooh is
a Bear of Enormous Brain."

Current and forthcoming titles from The Wisdom of Pooh

Pooh on Philosophy

The Tao of Pooh
by Benjamin Hoff

The Te of Piglet
by Benjamin Hoff

Pooh and the Philosophers
by John Tyerman Williams

Pooh and the Ancient Mysteries
by John Tyerman Williams

The Pooh Book of Quotations
Compiled by Brian Sibley

The Pooh Dictionary
by A.R. Melrose

Pooh on Management

Winnie-the-Pooh on Management
by Roger E. Allen

Winnie-the-Pooh on Problem Solving
by Roger E. Allen and Stephen D. Allen

Winnie-the-Pooh on Management & Problem Solving
in one paperback volume

Publishing in August 1998
Winnie-the-Pooh on Success
by Roger E. Allen and Stephen D. Allen

Pooh on Life

Pooh's Little Fitness Book
Inspired by A.A. Milne

Winnie-the-Pooh's Teatime Cook Book
Inspired by A.A. Milne

Winnie-the-Pooh's Trivia Quiz Book
Inspired by A.A. Milne

Eeyore's Gloomy Little Instruction Book
Inspired by A.A. Milne

Pooh's Little Instruction Book
Inspired by A.A. Milne

Latin Editions

Winnie ille Pu
by Alexander Lenard

Domus Anguli Puensis
by Brian Gerrard Staples

The Tao of Pooh
Benjamin Hoff
With original line drawings by E.H. Shepard

While Eeyore frets...
...and Piglet hesitates
...and Rabbit calculates
...and Owl pontificates
...Pooh just is.

Winnie-the-Pooh has a certain Way about him, a way of doing things which has made him the world's most beloved bear. And Pooh's Way, as Benjamin Hoff brilliantly demonstrates, seems strangely close to the ancient Chinese principles of Taoism.

The author's explanation of Taoism through Pooh, and Pooh through Taoism, shows that this is not simply an ancient and remote philosophy but something you can use, here and now.

Benjamin Hoff is a writer, photographer, musician and composer, and a specialist in Japanese fine-pruning, with a degree in Asian Art. He writes full-time. In his spare time he practises Taoist yoga and T'ai Chi Ch'uan. He lives in Portland, Oregon.

The Te of Piglet
Benjamin Hoff
With original line drawings by E.H. Shepard

In this sequel to *The Tao of Pooh*, author Benjamin Hoff explores the
Te (a Chinese word meaning Virtue) of the Small — a principle
embodied perfectly in Piglet. As delightful as it is instructive, *The Te
of Piglet* features dialogues between the author and the familiar
characters of Pooh, Eeyore, Tigger, Kanga and Baby Roo, and of
course, Piglet himself. These conversations are interspersed with
traditional Taoist stories and more than 50 illustrations from the
original Pooh books.

Combining the irresistible charm of A.A. Milne's classic stories,
the enduring wisdom of the ancient teachings, and the unique
contemporary appeal of its predecessor, *The Tao of Pooh*, this book
is sure to captivate the legions of readers who have found enlightenment
and pleasure in walking in the path of Pooh.

Pooh and the Ancient Mysteries
John Tyerman Williams
With original line drawings by E.H. Shepard

Pooh and the Ancient Mysteries reveals Winnie-the-Pooh as master of ancient lore and the supreme Magus of the coming of the Second Millennium. John Tyerman Williams explores A.A. Milne's classic stories, *Winnie-the-Pooh* and *The House at Pooh Corner,* to reveal fascinating hidden references to the Millennium, astrology, alchemy, hermetic philosophy, the Tarot, the Druids, I Ching, the Qabalah, and finally, the Female Mysteries which light the way to a Utopian society.

John Tyerman Williams proved in *Pooh and the Philosophers* that the whole of Western philosophy may be found in the stories of Winnie-the-Pooh. Now, as we move towards the end of the 20th century, he goes further to reveal the hermetic tradition sealed inside a honey jar.

John Tyerman Williams is a Doctor of Philosophy and a former actor and lecturer on theatre, English history and English literature. He lives in Tintagel, Cornwall, close to the birthplace of the Arthurian Legends.

Pooh and the Philosophers
John Tyerman Williams
With original line drawings by E.H. Shepard

This witty and elegant *jeu d'esprit* sets out to prove beyond all reasonable doubt that the whole of Western Philosophy, from the Cosmologists of Ancient Greece to the Existentialists of this century, may be found in *Winnie-the-Pooh* and *The House at Pooh Corner*. It shows how the Great Bear explains and illuminates the most profound ideas of the great thinkers, from Plato, Hume and Kant to Nietzsche, Heidegger and Sartre.

Even Winnnie-the-Pooh's most ardent fans may have hitherto underestimated his cosmic importance; this book will confirm however, once and for all, what many will have long suspected: that Pooh is a Bear of Enormous Brain.

John Tyerman Williams is a Doctor of Philosophy and a former actor and lecturer on theatre, English history and English literature. He lives in Tintagel, Cornwall.